The publisher of this book is generously donating all royalties from the retail sales of **"REMARKABLE HEALTH AND FITNESS"** to:

JUNIOR ACHIEVEMENT

Junior Achievement is the nation's largest organization dedicated to giving young people the knowledge and skills they need to own their economic success, plan for their futures, and make smart academic and economic choices.

Junior Achievement was founded in 1919 by Theodore Vail, president of American Telephone & Telegraph; Horace Moses, president of Strathmore Paper Co.; and Senator Murray Crane of Massachusetts. Its first program, *JA Company Program*®, was offered to high school students on an after-school basis.

In 1975, the organization entered the classroom with the introduction of Project Business for the middle grades. Over the last 39 years, Junior Achievement has expanded its activities and broadened its scope to include in-school and after-school students.

Junior Achievement reaches more than 4.8 million students per year in 209,651 classrooms and after-school locations. JA programs are taught by volunteers in inner cities, suburbs, and rural areas throughout the United States, by 109 Area Offices in all 50 states.

You can learn more about Junior Achievement by visiting:
http://JuniorAchievement.org

REMARKABLE HEALTH
AND FITNESS

REMARKABLE HEALTH AND FITNESS

Conversations with Leading Health, Nutrition and Fitness Professionals

VOLUME ONE

By Remarkable Press™

Remarkable Health and Fitness/ Mark Imperial. —1st ed.

Managing Editor/ Stewart Andrew Alexander

ISBN: 978-0-9987085-2-2

CONTENTS

A NOTE TO THE READER

Thank you for buying your copy of "Remarkable Health and Fitness: Conversations with Leading Health, Nutrition and Fitness Professionals." This book was originally created as a series of live interviews, that's why it reads like a series of conversations, rather than a traditional book that talks *at you*.

I wanted you to feel as though the participants and I are talking with you, much like a close friend, or relative and felt that creating the material this way would make it easier for you to grasp the topics and put them to use quickly.

So, rather than wading through hundreds of pages, grab a pen, take notes and get ready to learn some fascinating insights and real world experiences on health and fitness.

Warmest regards,

Mark Imperial
Author and Radio Personality

INTRODUCTION

"Remarkable Health and Fitness: Conversations with Leading Health, Nutrition and Fitness Professionals" is a collaborative book series featuring leading Fitness Professionals from across the country who are passionate about helping people to live healthy lifestyles.

Remarkable Press™ would like to extend a heartfelt thank you to all participants who took the time to submit their chapter and offer their support in becoming *'Get the word out Ambassadors'* for this project.

Remarkable Press™ has pledged 100% of the royalties from the retail sales of this book to be donated to Junior Achievement.

Should you want to make a direct donation, visit their website at: http://JuniorAchievement.org

MARYELLEN GROGAN

A Conversation with
C.P.T Maryellen Grogan
Owner of Positively Fit

Maryellen Grogan has been a Trainer since 1994 and owns and operates Positively Fit, in Maumee, Ohio.

Maryellen has expertise in post-rehabilitation, injury recovery, sports specific training (competitive and recreational) and women over 40. She integrates nutrition into her fitness programs for optimal progress and weight management.

During this interview, Maryellen discusses her exercise and nutrition program, designed to meet the unique needs of women over 40, especially perimenopause and menopause women.

Who's your ideal prospect Hanniel, who do you help?

Maryellen Grogan: The majority of our business is with the women over 40, mainly the perimenopausal, menopausal women.

Can you just share a few of the most common obstacles that prevent the women you work with from achieving their goals?

Maryellen Grogan: The number one that we see the most of is stress. Number two is there not eating enough, they think they have to starve themselves to lose weight. Number three would be that they either over exercise, or they don't exercise at all.

You talked about stress, can you just expand a little bit on that for us, please?

Maryellen Grogan: As we age, we have accumulation of stresses in our life, whether it's death, divorce, child rearing, and things like that. Those are all little straws on the camel's back. Then, as you start heading towards perimenopause, and menopause, your hormones start waning away, and that's another stressor, plus we live in a very, very toxic world, so toxics will cause stress. .

When women want to lose weight at this age, it's very difficult for them, because they don't understand that you have to look at stress, hormones, and toxins, all of it together, and along with the exercise portion.

You also mentioned the obstacle of not eating enough. Can you go a little deeper into that for us, please?

Maryellen Grogan: It's a common misconception for women to go low calorie in order to lose weight. They may see a weight loss on the scale, but it could be water weight, muscle weight, lean tissue, so we actually tell our clients not to get on a scale. I'd rather use our Bio Impendence tester which measures body fat, skeleton muscular, lean mass and water weight to name a few. Most women that we see do not eat enough calories throughout the day, along with not eating the proper foods.

The third obstacle you mentioned, was over exercising, or not exercising at all. Could you share some additional insights on that particular obstacle for us, please, Maryellen?

Maryellen Grogan: Our new clients have experienced the extreme ranges of either over exercising or not exercising at all, very seldom do we get a woman that comes in that does exercise at a moderate pace. They are either over exercising, for example doing hours of cardio, participated in extreme exercise class, or spinning class in an effort to lose the excess body fat, or, they're so confused about exercise, they don't exercise at all.

Can you name one or two examples?

Maryellen Grogan: Okay, a young woman came in, about 48 years old, she had excessive abdominal fat. This by the way is commonly associated with a prolonged stress response. She thought that, in order to get that body fat off, she would do a 3 times a week a hour long spinning class, then 2 to 3 times a week she would do a boot camp type of training. She was doing all those modalities of exercise; and was actually putting weight on.

What we did was backed her off all those type of exercises, had her do no aerobic whatsoever, and had her strength train only for a couple of months. We found out that her body recovered and adapted better with only 5 to 6 reps, moderate weight, and lots of rest in between each set. After a couple of months we had her do some leisurely walking on the off days, that was her so-called aerobic, but we kept her heart rate very low, no more than 100 beats per minute.

Then, we looked at her diet. The main thing for her was that she skipped breakfast. By skipping breakfast, her body had a chance to release insulin, and then she was off to the races with high insulin, low blood sugar, high insulin, low blood sugar.

We had her take a tablespoon of oil within 10 minutes of opening her eyes, 25 grams of protein, with lots of vegetables, and eating every 3 to 4 hours, vegetables and protein. By doing this, she didn't have those rapid blood sugar drops, and she was able to start losing some of that belly fat.

What we explained to her, too, that every time blood sugar drops, and insulin goes up, so does cortisol. Now, cortisol is a powerful hormone that we do need, but excessive cortisol has a lot of negative effects. One of the major effects is that it will put abdominal fat on. Then, we taught her how to meditate and how to do rhythmic breathing.

She used prayer as meditation on a daily basis and then she tried to get to bed by 10 at night, or even earlier, trying to get at least 7 to 8 hours sleep a night. With all these changes, she started seeing her energy getting better, her moods were getting better, and her clothes were fitting better, so she felt like she was starting to get her body back.

She wanted to address her hormonal issues, so we referred her to a Precision medicine doctor, who helped her replace some of the hormones naturally, that her body was not making anymore. Within about a year later, most of that belly fat came off. Now, starting at about the age of 45 and older it's not a quick fix. It takes a long time to undo all the damage that was done years prior, and we tell our clients that they need to be patient. They need to trust us, and be patient, and it usually works.

Just listening to that, Maryellen, it seems there's no such thing in your industry as a one size fits all. There's a real 360 degree approach to every individual person you work with. Am I on the right lines?

Maryellen Grogan: Yes, you are. Everybody has their own unique physiology, so you have to work with their physiology. My husband who is a certified nutritionist uses Hair Mineral Analysis, which is a blueprint of your physiology. The Hair Mineral Analysis also determines the metabolic type of his clients. This is very important to know about my client. Most of our client's metabolic type is either a fast or a slow.

A fast metabolic type is someone who gets in trouble very quickly, whether it's emotional or physical. For instance, if their blood sugar drops, it drops super-fast. These type of people have to eat about every three hours. If they are exercising, their body gets stressed very quickly. This stress reaction could be ten to hundreds times more than it should be. Exercise in itself is stress.

A slow metabolic type doesn't really stress very quickly, the blood sugar doesn't drop very fast, but they get out of trouble very slowly, so with these clients we can push a little bit more in the gym, but they have to rest more after their session. It could even mean they will need to take two or three days off from exercising before they go to the gym again. Our training is very specific. We train our clients according to their own unique physiology.

Let's talk a little bit about misconceptions.

Maryellen Grogan: The first one, I would say the number one misconception is they think they have to do a lot of aerobic or cardio activity. We hear often, "Well, it worked when I was in my twenties. I did a lot of cardio, and I lost the weight." Well, they don't have the hormone backup anymore to be able to train like that.

The second one is they think they have to keep their heart rates up to burn the most fat. Some of our new women were told that this will keep them in the fat burning zone. Well, keeping your heart rate up high for a good length of time actually stresses the body out more, and therefore, they end up putting body fat on.

The third misconception, once again, they think they have to go on a low calorie diet and eat hardly anything through the day just to lose weight.

Okay, Maryellen, let's take a step back to the point where you said, "People could actually get heavier by staying in the fat burning zone." Now, that sounds, contradictory to what one would normally think, so could you just expand on that for us, please?

Maryellen Grogan: All exercise is stress. Leisurely exercise or movement is not considered stress though. If your exercise intensity is high this type of exercise activates the sympathetic nervous system, which is fight. Our bodies are not made to be in fight or flight 24/7.

We have stressors all day long, driving, work, taking care of aging parents, emotional stress, nutritional stress, toxic stress to name a few and then when you go exercise, thinking you're going to release some of the stresses, yes, mentally you are, but physically you are not. You're adding more stress onto the body.

When you're in fight or flight, our bodies release a lot of cortisol. Cortisol is used for energy in all our cells. There are a lot of positive effects for cortisol, but not for excessive cortisol. What happens is, if you keep that heart rate up for a length of time, you're pushing your adrenals, then the adrenals just keep releasing more, and more, and more cortisol, which is a fat promoting hormone.

Women that are heading towards perimenopause or menopause, their bodies are more stressed reactive. We don't want to add more stress to it by exercising where their body can't adapt. That's the whole key.

When you're exercising continually in a higher heart rate, most women, I'm not saying all, most women don't adapt to it. They cannot recover from it, so therefore, they're stressing their adrenals, releasing too much cortisol, and putting weight on.

What we like to do is take them into fight or flight, with strength training, and then bring them out into parasympathetic. We've got a great little trick to bring our clients heart rates down faster. They sit on a stability ball, and we have them circle on it, roll on it.

They're actually massaging the sit bones and by doing this we can get them into a parasympathetic state, into a more rested state quicker. Once we see that their body has recovered, they will do the next exercise

Now, every individual is different. Our clients perform a lot of single leg exercises. Some of our women will have to sit after working just one leg before they go onto the other leg. That's how stressed their bodies are. Or, if we see that they are adapting and recovering, then we'll do both legs without resting in between.

We don't take our women into high heart rates anymore. For most of our women it's just too stressful to the body, keeping the heart rate up. Your adrenals make your heart beat, and you're just pushing the adrenals, which are already fatigued adrenals.

As you're heading towards menopause, the ovaries start shutting down, the adrenals take over to produce some of the hormones that the ovaries can't make anymore. If the adrenals are already too fatigued, they can't produce the needed hormones, so now you have an imbalance. The next best thing the body will do is put body fat on, because then it can get hormones from the body fat.

If you're toxic on top of that, that even stresses the body, and releases even more cortisol. What women have to understand is that it's not about low calories, getting in the fat burning zone, over training, it's about looking how you're adapting, how you're recovering, and what's my toxic level, what are my hormones doing, and am I resting enough?

This is contradictory to everything what you see in the media, is it not, Maryellen?

Maryellen Grogan: I'm sorry to say, but yes. But, what I'm saying though is that I am working with a population that doesn't have a strong hormonal base anymore. The 20 year olds, 30 year olds, yes, they can train hard, because they have that high testosterone, estrogen, progesterone and growth hormone which counteracts the damaging effects of all that exercise, but we are seeing more and more women in their 25's and 30's putting weight on from over training, they're releasing too much cortisol. I think it's mainly from toxicity.

We live in such a toxic world. In the year 2000, they said toxic chemicals had a 1000 increase since 1940s. If we get a toxic load, that disrupts hormones, it disrupts everything. They're finding toxics in the umbilical cords of infants.

I think the game has to change. I personally think the fitness industry is over training most of their participates. We can't train like that anymore. Our lifestyles are different, more stressful and our environment's different. I think people need to back off, and not train as hard. I think it's just pushing their adrenals too hard, and down the road, they're going to end up with issues.

What are some of the unknown pitfalls out there that 40 plus, 45 plus women, and older, who are going into the perimenopause, and menopause might not be aware of when they're wanting to get their bodies back?

Maryellen Grogan: Well, once again, it's stress. Stress just shows up everywhere. The baby boom generation especially the females thought and tried to do it all. I had a conversation in my studio with several of my clients about how we did it all, and we're like, "Well, how did that work out?" It stressed our bodies out.

The women having this conversation are the ones with the big bellies, that are having a hard time getting rid of the belly and we are the ones that had a horrible menopause. We all the ones that over trained in the past.

It's interesting. I guess we're just going to have to relearn our role in the world, as women about not trying to be all for everybody. Most women put themselves on the back burner, and everybody in front of them

We all are getting hit by stress, but of all the women I see, and believe me, I have seen many in the studio. The ones that are the most stressed are the overachievers. All of them over exercised while trying to do it all. These women had beautiful bodies until they hit menopause.

Is nutrition a part of the unknown pitfalls that are out there?

Maryellen Grogan: Yes. There's so much misconception about what good nutrition is, and what's not. Nutrition, as we age, has to be the number one priority. You cannot out train a bad diet. I tell my clients, they have to be 100% clean on their diet. That's the variable that they can control.

If they're not losing the weight, and their diet is super good, and this is what happened to me, then we have to look at hormones, cortisol, and toxicity. Nutrition is really important, that's why we send everybody to my husband, who's is the certified nutritionist. Very, very important.

When you think about the women you help, what are some of their most common fears about getting their bodies where they want them to be, while simultaneously experiencing perimenopause, and menopause?

Maryellen Grogan: The main fear is fear of failing. A lot of these women have done low calorie diets in the past, only to put more weight on afterwards. That's a common knowledge.

Then, they're so fearful of diet changes. They've had lifelong habits of eating certain foods, their comfort foods so they're so afraid that they cannot eat them again. That's the major one, is that diet change.

If there is somebody out there who's wanting to make a change and get their bodies back into shape, maybe one of their fears is what their family, friends, colleagues might say. Is that something that you come across, and can address?

Maryellen Grogan: You know what? You're absolutely correct on that. Yes. Because they will be doing something different than everybody around them, and they're afraid of what the other people are going to say to them. We find it, very often that it's a lot of time spouses sabotage, not on purpose, but just because the spouse doesn't want to change, so they sabotage the woman who's trying to make a change. It is a battle. It's tough. Especially families that make fun of them, because they're not eating the bread, or the pizzas, and things like that. You're correct on that, there is a fear there.

What would you say to those women who really want to make that change, but they're in an environment that's not conducive to the progress they are wanting to gain?

Maryellen Grogan: We always tell them, "Just take care of yourself first. You can't take care of anybody else if you're not feeling well, as well as you should." They just need to take care of themselves first, and shut the chatter down, do it for themselves.

Do you really enjoy what you do?

Maryellen Grogan: Oh, I love what I do. It's been my passion forever, and the more I know, the less I know. I'm constantly educating, and changing, and being open-minded to anything I can do to help my clients. My passion is to get them better, to help them.

This sounds like an obvious question, but why would these 40 plus, 45 plus and older women want to get their bodies back, as they're going through perimenopause and menopause?

Maryellen Grogan: It's basically vanity. I mean, every woman wants to look good, fit in smaller size clothes, and to be healthy, and vibrant, and strong. As you start going through perimenopause, and menopause, you don't feel vibrant anymore, you don't feel strong anymore.

The weight starts creeping up, and you look in the mirror, and you think, "What happened to me?" They just want to drop some weight, get back to that strong, vibrant self. What woman doesn't want to feel that way?

Let's talk about some of the domino effects of not getting their bodies back into shape. Can you expand on some of those points that you mentioned of feeling tired, having low moods and excess fat? What are some of the long term domino effects if they don't actually do something about that?

Maryellen Grogan: Well, the top 10 medications sold in this country are all related to symptoms, and diseases associated with stress.

The number one reason why everyone goes to the doctor is because of stress related symptoms, such as fatigue. As a woman starts going through the change, everything is out of whack, so this is the time that proper nutrition is a must, women have to eat clean. This is the time that, if you are working out, you have to make sure that you're training where you're recovering and adapting to the stress of exercise.

Losing the excess body fat is actually more achievable through balancing out our hormones through Bioidentical hormones. Not everybody believes in Bioidentical hormones. There's tons of research out there that says how beneficial it is. I tend to be a believer in it, I am on Bioidentical hormones, because I want to feel good, and have a long, healthy life.

Now, if women start going through perimenopause, and menopause, and they're still eating horrible, they're not addressing stress, they're going to even start seeing decreased bone density, decreased muscle, high blood pressure, inflammatory response goes up, blood sugar is all over the place, they might become insulin resistant, thyroid function goes down, along with memory function going down. These are all the things that could happen if a woman doesn't really start taking care of herself as she starts going through the change.

Then, it's not only the effect it has on her, but the direct effect it has on others around her such as her family members, her job, her community, the list just goes on and on, this is a huge domino effect.

Maryellen Grogan: Exactly. This could affect the relationship with their significant other. The sex drive is not there, that's not a good thing for a marriage. When a woman is going through these stages, you know, they're irritable, tired, quick-tempered, depressed. Getting their diets under control and hormones more balanced could make a huge impact on how a woman feels. It does affect everybody around them.

Share, for a few minutes, your back story, and how it relates to the people you help.

Maryellen Grogan: Through my whole life, I have always been an athlete, and very fit, and actually very thin. When I started hitting perimenopause, I put on 80 pounds very quickly. I can relate to these women that are going through this, because I'm going through it.

I ended up going to several Precision medicine doctors, and they all threw their hands up, they didn't know what to do with me, so I started researching along with help from my husband to figure out why I put on so much weight and why it is so hard to get it off. The main reason was stress. By working with my husband, doing many hair mineral analysis, I was probably what they call sympathetic dominant my whole life. That's why I was so thin. It worked for me back then, that means I had high cortisol, high adrenalin which made me have a lot of energy, so then, I over trained for many years

When I hit the perimenopause, and put on all that weight, I thought, okay, I'm going to train this weight off. Well, guess what, I kept putting more, and more weight on. I finally, found a doctor who worked with my hormones, I did a powerful detox program to get the toxics out of me, and learned how to exercise where I can at least adapt to it, mediated daily, took daily naps and rested whenever I could. I was able to drop about 55 pounds of that added weight.

It had nothing to do with my diet, it all had to do with high cortisol, so now it's even tougher to get the weight off, but I understand. But I'm still strong, and I'm still vibrant after going through hormone replacement, and learning how to train right, so my whole passion now is to help women like myself, to help them understand what they're going through, and how they can switch it around.

That's basically my story. I'm almost 60 years old, and I don't plan retiring from training for at least another 10 years or more, because I love it so much. I know there are a whole lot of women out there I need to help out.

What would be your best piece of advice to those 40, 45 plus-year-old women, and older, who are going to that period of life, shortly before the occurrence of perimenopause, and menopause, and are not only considering, but wanting to get their bodies back? What would you like to share with them, Maryellen?

Maryellen Grogan: First, and foremost, get your diet really clean. Get on a really good nutritional program, eat good quality proteins, fats and lots of vegetables.

Second, try anyway you can to lower stress levels. Be aware when your body's stressed. We have taught our women how to be aware of that. Learn how to meditate, learn how to rhythmic breathe, any way to get that stress level down. Do not over train. You are not 20 and 30 years old anymore. You cannot train like you did back then. You need to back off on the training, eat more and train less. Strength train in moderation

Leisurely walking, leisurely swimming, leisurely biking, but make sure it's leisurely. Don't think you have to push yourself.

Then, the last is, get some sleep. You need to sleep. During this change for women, sleep is really tough, but if your cortisol is too high from being too stressed throughout the day, and if your diets not good, it's going to make the sleep patterns even worse. Take naps when you need to, especially on the weekends, or if you have an opportunity during the day, go have a nap, and don't feel bad about it. Give yourself permission.

Does any of this apply to males as well?

Maryellen Grogan: Yes, it does. Men shouldn't over train, also. They need to be able to adapt to the stress of exercise, they need to rest. There's male menopause, low testosterone, so forth. Men are toxic, just like females are. This does apply to them, also.

If the reader wants to know more, how would they be able to connect with you, Maryellen?

Maryellen Grogan: They can go to my website, its http://BePositivelyFit.com, and there's a section on the home page, where they can sign up for my newsletter or they can just bypass the website, and then just email me at BePositivelyFit@gmail.com.

Excellent, I love that name by the way, BePositivelyFit, very simple, and to the point.

Maryellen Grogan: Thank you.

Maybe there's a question I didn't ask you, or maybe there's a golden nugget that you want to share before we wrap things up... your final thoughts, please.

Maryellen Grogan: I'll end with one of my favorite quotes which I love, "If you don't take care of your body where are you going to live?"

BRIAN BOYLE

A Conversation with Doctor of Physical Therapy, Brian J. Boyle, PT, DPT of Company5k, LLC

For the past 19 years, Brian J. Boyle has been providing cost-effective, proven solutions to increase employee participation in health and wellness activities.

During this conversation, Brian discusses some of the common obstacles, misconceptions and unknown pitfalls employers face when trying to increase employee participation in health and wellness activities in order to reduce healthcare costs from the bottom line.

Who's your ideal prospect Brian, who do you help?

Brian Boyle: A great prospect is the employer that is looking for some creative ways to generate bottom line revenue. Quite often employers sit around and they'll say, "Hey, how do we get more profit? How do we add to our bottom line?" I see this happen all the time. What I do is I help those employers with reducing their employees' health and wellness costs and that, in return, adds to the bottom line in revenue.

Share two to three of the common obstacles that prevent them from reducing their bottom line spending on their employees' health and wellness.

Brian Boyle: One of the biggest struggles employers face is trying to do this themselves. By this, I mean putting together a health and wellness "program" or initiative, in-house on their own.

These companies are devoting tremendous amounts of resources, whether it's staffing, money, space, you name it, which can be better utilized elsewhere. Think about it, that same amount of resources could be put into their marketing, sales, research and development, whatever it may be, instead of trying to reinvent the wheel to come up with a program. By hiring an outside consultant or organization trained in Corporate Health and Wellness to come in and set up a program, the employer saves time, energy and money.

How these programs often start in-house is by a company relying on or looking to employees who either bring them the idea or who are what is commonly referred to as the "office champions." They're the ones that come up with the idea or who have a "passion" for motivating others around them. They may not have any training but more of a desire.

Either way, these employees will quite often say to management, "Hey, you know, we'd love to start a program," to which the employer replies, "This sounds great. Can you put together a committee and come up with something for us?"

But these employees don't really have the expertise in program design and so what you end up getting is a haphazard program or at worst, some initiative with no systems in place and over time if that person leaves the program is left hanging.

Another common obstacle seen, and this one is quite interesting, is a lot of employees don't like working out in their office but this usually isn't known until after a fitness center is built at work. A recent trend is showing where larger employers are converting space and adding a fitness "center." Some are gigantic, fully loaded gyms and others may have a few pieces of equipment and some free weights.

These employers may have personal consultants coming in, coaches or personal trainers, to assist their employees on a 1 on 1 basis. Now there is nothing wrong with this, if it aligns with the company culture. In that case, it's fine and the employees will actually benefit from this type of approach. Depending on the industry though, there is a large percentage of people who still look at their work space, as their "work." Because of the negative connotation, or maybe the feelings of not liking what they do, they don't want to add one more thing to their work day, like "working out" on campus.

So you'll go to these large companies who have these beautiful fitness centers and you'll see very few people actually in there working out. This drives employers crazy and they sit down and say, (only after they have already built the facility), "Well, gosh, what did we do wrong?" Then they start talking to their employees and what seemed like a good idea previously may not be a great idea after all.

They hear their employees say things like, "You know, I see so-and-so, my co-worker or my boss, for eight to ten hours a day already. I don't want to see them for another hour, okay?" Time already spent at work is another big reason. The greater the amount of hours already working the less likely the employee will want to "stick around" to workout, no matter how the employer tries to incentivize them. This is especially true for parents who may already feel guilty for being away long hours from their families. They don't want to take another 30-60 minutes, even if they know it is for their own health.

And that leads to the next common obstacle. Many employers do not have the right incentives in place for their health and wellness programs. Incentives can be monetary.

They can be time off or flex scheduling. They could be fitness related products like wearable fitness trackers or certificates for new shoes and so on. Whatever the incentive is, it comes down to company culture. If the incentives aren't aligned with the values and beliefs of the existing employees, then the employer is going to see some big issues. In this instance, even with the best designed program or systems offered, their employees may not want to participate.

The final obstacle I'd like to share is the disconnect between what executive teams say and what they actually do. In instances like that, it causes be a big problem. If the executive team says, "Hey, we're going to put this program into place," and yet they themselves are overweight and or not taking care of themselves the initiative won't work. Or if they are working long hours and not participating in the program themselves, you again have a recipe for disaster.

Think about it this way, if an employee is being told that they are going to need to work overtime and the executive team says, "You know, we really want you to work out. Um, try to find time on your own time in the, you know, in the other 12 hours that you're off," and they themselves are not living healthy, it just won't happen. The average employee will find any excuse they can to not work out because again there is a disconnect between the message and the program intentions/company culture.

Share an example of how you've been able to help one of your clients to overcome one of those three obstacles that you've just mentioned.

Brian Boyle: One of my clients in the commercial transportation industry has been able to overcome many of the obstacles I just mentioned. Commercial transportation companies face many of the barriers that we just talked about and they are an interesting client to work with because they've got a remote workforce; with employees working all across the United States. When you think about that, the difficulties of trying to get a remote workforce together on anything whether it's health and wellness, compliance, same policies and procedures, you name it, it's an uphill battle.

One of the big barriers faced by drivers especially, which can be faced by the office associates as well, is what they would perceive as time and/or the space limitations. Most trucking companies don't have massive and/or elaborate operating centers. Those who do may only have one or two of their centers which are large and then they may have smaller satellite centers with employees but not many amenities. So because of this perceived "lack of space" you have to be creative in providing programs. Imagine being in the cab of a tractor trailer where you have a bunk, some storage space, and two seats. Most people would not picture themselves being able to exercise in there.

What we were able to do for the drivers was work with them to start seeing their truck as an area they could workout in or around. By either putting exercise equipment into their trucks or showing them how they could do something like walk 50 laps around the cab and trailer to equal a mile, we showed them that often times what they saw as a perceived barrier was only that... perceived.

We started by providing information. And this is key. The conversation would often go something like this, "Hey, you know what? You don't need a whole lot of equipment and you actually have a break throughout the day in your drive time. What other things do you like doing and can we get you to do those in that down time?" And it's amazing because after that conversation they would see things differently. We were able to break them, and not all of them mind you, but a majority of them of their old self-limiting beliefs.

We also had to question why some things were being done in a certain way. It turned out there were some policies and procedures we had to change in order to make some of these healthy changes for the drivers. We worked with the upper management, who because of a caring company culture were very willing to make adjustments which would help their drivers.

So in order to allow things like weights and exercise equipment in the cab we had to change a policy which was in place which prohibited workout equipment, like dumbbells in the cab. Another policy which had to be changed allowed for drivers to strap their bicycle to the back of the cab. Prior to our discussion things like this had not been allowed and had been seen as a liability.

So at the end of the day, it really came down to that top-down approach and to company culture. The incentives were there and they were aligned with the values of the organization and what the employees wanted. The client started incentivizing through a wellness program that was available to all drivers. We were providing coaching through phone. They also had a nurse health hotline that they can call into if they had any questions and concerns.

This all worked great because we are a third party, they didn't tie up their resources in-house, trying to figure out how to change their employees' health. We were able to put programs on throughout the year, so anytime somebody stopped into one of the operating centers for the trucking company, we could actually sit down with these individuals, coach them, then we'd mark down that we had this instruction and then we'd enter into a database.

Really, the turnaround was astronomical when you think of normally a sedentary population. Within the first couple of years, this company saw close to a 24-to-1 return on investment. That's pretty huge. Now, again, they're more of an extreme case of what is possible. Most people will see around a 2-to-1 to a 3-to-1 return on their investment for dollars spent on health and wellness but I think this is a really good example of an industry in which it would be very easy to just say things will never change and that it can't be done. It just takes this team approach and reducing these barriers and you can actually see a significant decrease on bottom line spend.

When you think about the people you serve, can name one or two of the most common misconceptions that hold them back?

Brian Boyle: Yeah, absolutely. One of the misconceptions is that it's going to cost a lot to improve health. This is a really big misconception in the sense that the employers are often only thinking, "We've either got to spend money to save money," or "Spend money to make money." In reality that type of thinking is self-limiting, it doesn't actually cost a lot to improve health.

Some of the things that we talked about, reducing the barriers of access to the healthy options can go really a long way without actually costing a whole heck of a lot. And better yet, there is generally a return on investment when run well. What does it really cost to improve the company culture by having the discussion to find out what employees actually want and why health is so important?

After that it comes down to educating the employees. That doesn't cost anything. Literally, other than some time, which again you can come back to the time is money concept but if you're thinking about from the spend perspective, you can do that and then hire that out or outsource that out to somebody else once you figure out what it is you want.

Another misconception is that access equals knowledge. I find this fascinating and it's almost counter intuitive to most. A lot of employers now offer their employees a monthly stipend to join a gym. Whether it is through their health insurance or the employer themselves we are seeing this trend more and more. And yet when you ask how many employees actually participate the number is ridiculously low.

Most companies have like a 26% participation rate in their physical fitness programs (including gym membership subsidy). When we're talking to employees and we will ask why they are not participating in their employers gym membership program, they quite often say, "Well, I, I don't know what to do when I get there."

Unfortunately a lot of employers pat themselves on the back because they crossed off an item on the list when they never really asked the employees what they wanted in the first place. And just because an employee has a membership doesn't mean they know the proper way to exercise to maximize not only their time but their results as well. And so you end up with access and no instruction and the compliance drops off exponentially.

Another thing is that not all employees actually want to improve their health. I know that sounds strange and you would almost have to ask, "Why wouldn't somebody want to improve their health?" Honestly, there's a lot of reasons, and we could go into a lot of different variables. At the end of the day, there are going to be those employees who just do not want to improve. Their status quo is where they want to be. Maybe they tried something in the past because they were given the opportunity. Maybe it was a contest that was run by the employer in the past and they didn't win. Maybe it was that the incentives were wrong. It could be that they just didn't know what they were doing. They started a walking program, didn't lose any weight, and so they think, "Why would I do that again?"

The behavioral modification component is a big key in the health and wellness. Yeah, I think those are some of the biggest misconceptions and myths. That the people want to be healthy, that everything is costly, and/or that if you provide somebody access, that they're going to know exactly what to do.

Are there any other misconceptions that you come across out there, Brian?

Brian Boyle: Probably another one is that wellness programs are just not fun. They're not all equal and sometimes employees don't participate because they just don't connect with the activity or they don't see how it relates to them. We come across this quite often when there's something like the "Maintain, Don't Gain Challenge." This is one of my favorites, and I'm being sarcastic when I say this.

But around the holidays, between Thanksgiving and Christmas, a lot of companies run a program in which it is okay to maintain, even your unhealthy weight, as long as you don't gain anymore. Well, that doesn't sound like a whole lot of fun. It's almost like the participation trophy for healthy living. I can maintain my ridiculously unhealthy lifestyle just as long as I don't let it get any worse. I mean, c'mon how does that even promote health?

You want to make sure that you're including some sort of fun, whether it's through gamification and tracking activity on a leaderboard or something along the lines of making it a little bit of a competition. You just have to remember that not everybody's driven by competition and that everybody's definition of fun is going to be different as well.

It's always difficult when you're dealing with the human variable, with people, and trying to figure out what they want and what's going to work best. Sometimes you end up having to put a program out there that may not hit everybody in the same way, and then you've got to try and figure out how do you not exclude people either.

You want to make sure that everybody has an availability to participate even if some don't want to. Actually, there's laws that now say that you can't incentivize to the exclusion of certain people so everybody's got to have equal opportunity to become involved by law, but it doesn't mean everyone will and sometimes you just have to accept that.

Is there a misconception that access equals knowledge?

Brian Boyle: Yeah, there really is. I'll give you another example. Say you have an office chair and your office chair has about 10 different adjustments on it. This is especially true in real high-end office chairs. You can adjust the seat stem up and down, you can adjust the seat back, you can adjust the arms up and down, in and out, the tilt on the seat pan and so on.

Employers will have this false belief that because they spent all this money on these chairs, their employees must be comfortable. And they never ask and then they can't figure out why people still aren't at maximum productivity and why they are still missing time from work for pain. And yet you talk to the employees and ask how many of them know all of the seat adjustment capabilities and it is only a small percentage of them at most.

Again, even though they may have the top of the line equipment at their disposal, if no one has ever come by to show them how to use their chair or they have never taken the time to figure it out themselves, they will not know how to use it and all of those fancy features are wasted.

You'll also find this in the realm of health and fitness when you talk about diet and exercise. These two things, diet and exercise, are just as prescriptive as any other medication for conditions like type 2 Diabetes, Cardiovascular Disease, and Stroke. A lot of people don't want to go on medications but they just don't know any other way.

The problem is not that they don't have access to healthy foods but they don't know what to eat or what time to eat or how much or how little to eat. They could have a gym membership or a fitness center on-site at the employer but yet don't know how to maximize the workout to be effective.

In reality, it is very easy to become paralyzed with this fear of not knowing what to do or how to do it right because, if you don't do this or if you don't do that, you'll actually do something wrong. This is a real fear that people come up with. They start to analyze things to the point that they don't even know where to start and so they don't.

Another interesting thing is, and this isn't a knock against the primary care physician because they are the cornerstone of healthcare but the "check with your physician before you exercise" moniker really came out of a marketing piece that the primary care physicians were doing and has only been in existence for the last 50 or so years.

From a legal standpoint, It's a great medical disclaimer to say check with your physician first but what it's quite often seen as is just another barrier. The physicians will tell you everyone should be seen prior to changing their routine or starting a new one and yet, in reality, everybody should be exercising. This was great when everyone was working manually and getting physical activity.

We know that there's these benefits to exercise and yet people will become paralyzed because they saw on the bottom of a workout video that it says, "Consult with your physician before starting any new activity," and I don't have time to get into my doctor's office or I don't have the money right now so they don't go and they don't start.

Again, It's not a personal knock against the physicians but I really feel like unless you have a medical condition which you are currently being treated for all of us should be able to perform some time of physical activity and that this disclaimer really only adds to place another barrier in the front of the people who may need physical activity the most.

Brian, when employers communicate with their employees, they are hearing one thing. However, you are hearing something completely different. Is that what happens on a regular basis?

Brian Boyle: This is an interesting topic. When third parties come in to the worksite, they can sometimes act as a buffer between the employee and the employer. Employees are quite often more willing to open up with their true feelings if they believe that what they say will not be directly linked to them and get back to their employer.

In general, even the most pessimistic employees, who believe nothing will ever change, will tell a third party what they think even if they have given up on the employer ever changing. It's almost like, well, a fresh set of ears which makes employees feel like they can provide that honest discussion about what they're looking for and why things haven't maybe worked in the past. And since there's no repercussions coming from saying something, the discussions can become really quite candid.

But again, it does come down to the culture of the company. If the employer has an open space concept, we're seeing a lot more of this in tech companies in where nobody really has a cubicle, it seems like everyone is more open to sharing and getting involved. In those situations, there's a little bit more open and honest discussion already taking place.

In other cases where there may be some distrust between employee and senior level management you will quite often see a disconnect and less open and honest communication. Try to put a health and wellness plan in place and it will fail miserably.

But it's not always just the employees. Sometimes mid-level managers, will get great ideas from their employees but they are too afraid to stick their necks out and risk disruption of the status quo. If something fails, it's their neck on the line, and so you'll get a lot of these really, really good ideas that may come up but just never actually take hold, depending on the company culture.

When it comes to reducing employee health and wellness cost, what are one or two known pitfalls that the individuals and organizations you work with may not be aware of, Brian? Can you share one or two of those with us please?

Brian Boyle: Yeah. Great question. One of the pitfalls that I see is that right now, the insurance providers are looking at ways to keep their customers, which employers make up currently, the second-largest group of insured individuals in the United States. If you think about the pool of number of covered lives, companies make up this second-largest group, and so they've got a big say in what they want.

The insurers understand that and they want these companies covered by their particular insurance. They want to cover as many lives as possible, and so if you've got an organization that has 5,000 employees, well, that's a real easy way to go and get 5,000 additional covered lives for that insurance provider. All they do is go to the employer, rather than trying to advertise on television and go out to the mass media marketing and trying to get 5,000 people to sign up through their insurance benefits.

The problem though is that these insurance providers will often offer their own "wellness programs." And let's use wellness programs loosely here, because they will quite often times attempt to provide a one size fits all approach and their programs will quite often miss the mark on increasing employee participation rates.

For an example, quite often times insurance companies will offer what's known as an HRA. HRA stands for Health Risk Assessment. These lengthy assessments will ask hundreds of questions in an attempt to fully understand your full risk of developing certain conditions. How they incentivize the employee to participate is by either offering to reduce their insurance premium, by providing money into a health savings account or by just providing a gift certificate of some sort to get participation numbers up.

Health risk assessments are only one type of offering in a wellness program, however. And while, there's nothing wrong with health risk assessments we almost have to go back to that point of access equaling knowledge. Once an employee takes a health risk assessment and has the results they need to know what to do next. It's not enough to tell someone they have high cholesterol they need to know how to manage it or reduce it.

The same goes for someone who realizes they are 50 lbs. overweight but doesn't know what they need to change to drop the additional weight. So there has to be some sort of system in place to be able to not only follow up with the employee but to also help guide them to reach their end goal.

But let's get back to the point of insurance providers and why they don't make great resources for making changes in health. The insurance providers will provide coverage for many different industries, with many different employers and across many different company cultures. It's very difficult to actually put in place a one-size fits everyone program in every one of their clients.

And quite honestly, they don't really have a desire to. It's not their main business line and there's no incentive for the insurance provider to offer this service for their covered clients. They offer these things as a "benefit" and the employer is sold on the fact that they may be able to lower their insurance premiums if they get their employees to participate. But there is no guarantee. And at the end of the day, there's really no incentive for the insurance providers to offer wellness programs at this point.

Another pitfall is when the employers go out and hire a wellness coach or a personal trainer for every single employee. Not only does this get really costly really quickly, but it is also a shotgun approach which does not target the group of people who need the personal service the most. It comes down to offering the same thing, a "one size fits nobody" package, quite honestly, to every single employee.

It'd be like getting every single employee the same office chair, even though you have employees that are 6 foot 5 and maybe weight 150 pounds and then you'd get somebody that is 5 foot 2 and may weigh 250 pounds. Those two individuals are going to need completely different chairs to feel comfortable.

Why is hiring a personal wellness coach or personal trainer for every single employee not a great idea? Say you have an employee who, has no desire to become healthier. Maybe they've got some sort of disability or medical condition that would preclude them from participating in the program or they don't like working out at work, now what you've done is you've added an entirely new cost for something that was basically a problem looking for a solution, not the other way around.

Those are probably two of the biggest pitfalls that I've seen from working in the trenches. That these employers will get sold on these ideas and they think they sound great and yet may not be effective. Somebody's a very good salesperson or they've got a good relationship connection and, in reality, it benefits the person who sold the employer on this benefit much more so than it does the actual employer or the employee.

When you think about the CEOs and the organizations, the corporate, the HR directors that you speak with on a daily basis, what are some of their most common fears about even attempting to reduce employee health and wellness costs?

Brian Boyle: I've been doing this for almost 19 years now, when I talk to these HR managers and the CEOs and the CFOs and COOs, the entire executive teams they quite often have reservations about adding "non-revenue" producing programs and initiatives even if there is potential for return on investment. They have lots of questions and my job is to then guide them through the process of starting a program and looking at both direct and indirect costs associated with wellness programs.

One of the biggest fears is change. Quite often times I hear prospective clients say, "We've tried something already," or, "We have something already in place," so they won't even look at new options... If the program is relatively new, they will want to take a wait and see approach instead of asking the tough questions like, "is what we are doing working?"

A perfect example of this is when I recently spoke with the Vice President of Human Resources for a large tech company. I called her to talk to her about some health and wellness programs and to see if we could help to provide them a solution. This VP told me that they already had some things they were doing.

When I asked her for specifics she mentioned they already sponsor something like 15 different employee softball teams and they have health coaches coming out to talk to their employees. She told me she was not interested in looking at any other options at the moment because she really did not feel that they had a health issue with any of their employees and all that they did already was costing them money.

In an example like the above scenario the senior level executive had no long term vision for their health and wellness and was merely allocating resources on a first-come, first-served basis. They also typically only see an increase in short term costs instead of looking at the long term value-add, which would therefore require a change in her thinking.

Companies will quite often only look at the immediate spend and not look at the long term and the savings of direct and the indirect costs. Savings in indirect costs, like turnover and poor health/low productivity, can sometimes be as much as three times of direct costs and the savings alone would pay for the right solution to their health and wellness needs.

If the tech firm is hiring mostly young, healthy individuals already, it may not be an issue. As those young, healthy individuals continue to age, there's going to be certain things that may come to bear with that. It'll be interesting.

Lastly, some companies may be in growth mode at the moment and so while they know they ought to be doing something they don't have the resources of either time, talent, or money to get a program started. And health and wellness just kind of gets put off.

It sounds like an obvious question by why would an employer want to reduce the costs on their employees' health and wellness, Brian?

Brian Boyle: If we put it into actual dollars, let's say you as a company want to earn a conservative 10% net profit this year. That's a good goal for a lot of companies. If you were selling a million dollars' worth of product and you wanted 10% profit, well that's $100,000. If you as the employer can save a $100,000 in healthcare costs, there's the same 10% in growth.

The upside is that you as the employer didn't have to sell anything more than you already were. You didn't have to go out and find more customers. You literally utilized the resources you either have at their disposal as an employer or worked with someone who does, to change the bottom line through becoming healthier.

But let's now talk about the converse of that to really hammer the point home. Say the same company wants to make 10% profit and they have an accident at work where someone is really hurt bad. Then let's say the medical costs for the company go up by $100,000 in the course of the year. In order to make the same 10% profit the company will now need to increase their revenue by an additional $1 million dollars. So now they need $2 million in revenue just to cover the additional expense of health care spend. So it really does make a significant difference.

What it all boils down to really is the company's ability to manage and control the things within their power to control. At a minimum, programs need to reduce injuries and/or improve health and be able to show a positive return on investment.

You absolutely love doing this, don't you, Brian? I really feel your passion coming through. Is this something that you really enjoy doing?

Brian Boyle: Absolutely, yes. I love solving problems, helping others, and anything to do with health and fitness. I am always telling others if I had gotten into my line of work, I honestly don't know what I would be doing right now. As a professional, helping people and really making change and seeing the changes is rewarding.

If you're doing something and you're not seeing an immediate benefit, you can really start to question how much impact you have. What I do really, I feel, honestly makes a difference in my clients. It really does.

Could you just share a little bit about your backstory?

Brian Boyle: Absolutely. I got into physical therapy with the desire to help others. I mean, literally, that's it. I also wanted to work with people and make them feel better and I've always been a people pleaser, so that helps in my line of work. Through my physical therapy career and working with employers, I started a company called Company5K, LLC to provide cost-effective and proven solutions for reducing costs for employers. What I really I really wanted to do was change how and why employees participate in the fitness programs offered by their employers.

Historically employers have about a 26% participation rate in their employees taking advantage of their health and wellness programs. An engagement rate that low means something is not working.

One service Company5K, LLC provides for employers is a turnkey health and wellness solution focused on physical activity through walking and running. In high school I started running and then ran in college and continued running after my college career. I enjoy running so much I even did my Doctoral work on running related injuries. So I thought what if I could combine my passion for running and my knowledge about running related injuries and health and wellness to help employers? So I did.

We developed a 12-week fitness program that costs nothing more to participate in than entry into our live event, a 5K run/walk Corporate Challenge and a 1-mile run. We use the crowdsourced concept to fund the races and put on an event bigger than any one company would want to try to put on by themselves.

How it works: To start our 30+ page manual is given to every person who signs up for the race. The manual takes the runner through everything they would need to know and this works really well for first timers especially. So to start a running coach has provided, a beginner, an intermediate program, and an advanced program so that, from day one, each person knows exactly what they're doing.

Then we have a nutritionist who put together meal plans based on the calories burned in each of the workouts put together by the running coach. Because diet is so important to overall health this was a must in the program.

Then I talk about injury prevention and provide examples of what to expect. For an example, when you start feeling pain at week 5, this is what you're going to want to do try ice massage and so on.

Then we have a sports psychologist, talking about behavior modification. How do you fit the exercise routine into your day if you're already stressed? How do you fit this into this back of your brain where you've said, "Nothing has worked before? Why would I try this?" We need this behavior modification piece as well for motivation and support. It ends in a large culminating event in Downtown Salt Lake City on a Thursday night, right after work. We do a 5K and we do a 1-

mile run or walk called, Company Cup 5K and the Wasatch Mile. These events allow the employee to self-pace their activity over the 12 weeks leading up to the event and then participate in an event that is on a weekday. The weekday is important because it reduces that barrier where people might think twice about getting out of bed on a Saturday morning.

That's kind of our solution that we started doing now and starting to see some really key success with this. It all came out from wanting to find a way to help people change the activity that we know is so important to their overall health and wellness and their well-being.

What would be your best piece of advice to professionals out there considering reducing their employee healthcare costs then, Brian?

Brian Boyle: I think one of the big pieces is that you've got to consider and understand the company culture first and foremost. And then you need to make sure that the executive team is committed to success. Whether it's a company that has 10 individuals or it's a company that has 10,000 individuals, it doesn't matter. Company Culture is going to be key. Don't just guess. Ask the employees directly what they want and then try to give them what they want.

I think that's where you see the real downside of wellness program implementation. It becomes one more thing on a checklist of too many things already, and so that's the best of advice is literally make sure that whatever program you put in is right for the company culture and that you have that executive team buy-in. Then and only then will you going to end up with a successful program and you're going to end up with a healthy, viable workforce that is going to help your bottom line.

Do you have any final thoughts that you'd like to share?

Brian Boyle: Absolutely. There's a lot of good discussions going on right now about corporate health and wellness; and I believe there needs to be. I always look in forums and online and in the business journals and such and you're seeing these good articles and good discussion, but much of the information sounds good but in reality does little to do more than just make people feel good.

It doesn't actually move the needle on health and bottom line spending, so you've got to really look through the weeds to say, "What is the correct information that's out there?" Do your research, talk to your employees about what their interests and know your company culture.

At the end of the day, look for ways to increase physical activity! Whether it's yourself or for your employees, get moving. It could be through flex scheduling, it could be fitness programs, covering costs for 5K races or even for sports league participation. Just be sure not to make it so haphazard that you can't figure out if it's actually moving the needle on health.

Not only will, your employees or you be healthier, but they're going to be more productive. They're going to be more engaged and they're likely to stick around a lot longer than they might traditionally at another employer.

How can people connect with you, Brian?

Brian Boyle: Company Cup is a 12-week training program, we implement our corporate wellness programs based around physical activity, running and walking, because we feel that everybody has access to those.

If you would like more information about these programs, feel free to reach out to me. My phone number is 801-447-1063. You can also visit the website, which is www.company5k.com, or you can even send me an email at brian@company5k.com and I'll be happy to get you as much information as you'd like.

DANIEL POLLACCIA

A Conversation with Daniel Paul Pollaccia
Martial Arts Instructor/Personal Trainer of
Mastermind Martial Arts & Fitness

Daniel Pollaccia owner/operator of Mastermind Martial Arts and Fitness in Victorville, California has been in martial arts since 2001, and the fitness industry since 2006.

He enjoys helping anyone that wants to get in better shape, whether through martial arts or one of his fitness programs.

Daniel has a very analytical approach to training which helps his clients achieve results through structured training sessions.

During this conversation, Daniel talks about teaching and training other who want to reach their fitness, competition, or self-defense goals.

Who's your ideal prospect Hanniel, who do you help?

Daniel Pollaccia: People tend to be intimidated. They walk into a big gym like 24 Hour Fitness or Planet Fitness because those gyms have millions of dollars of marketing behind them it's what the average person sees on a daily basis. But what the average person forgets is that those gyms, they're all about sales and stuff.

There is little personal investment on the gyms end of it. I used to go to places like that myself and they're quite intimidating. They're always trying to up sell on something and not everyone's made of money. Having enough money for a membership but then they try to sell you towel service and all this other stuff that's really unnecessary. It's just to make extra money. They don't have the fitness of people in mind. It's all about numbers and meeting quotas.

Could you just spend a few minutes explaining two to three common obstacles that prevent your clients getting into better shape?

Daniel Pollaccia: Obstacles come in many forms. Sometimes budget is a limitation. With my prices, I keep them the same all across the board and if people do package deals with me or want more, they pay more up front, I'll actually knock money off. I'm very affordable and that's, I think, the first obstacle that people come across is money.

I want to be paid for my time but I'm not so obsessed with it that I'm going to charge an exorbitant amount that people can't afford or if they can afford it, they can only afford it for a lesson here and there. A lot of places are $60 to $100 an hour depending on where you live with those kind of prices, you know, how much someone really going to train with you? How much disposable income do they really have?

I think the first obstacle is price to some people and then lack of knowledge. People want to take the first step but they don't know how to take that first step and where to start to get on that path to fitness. A lot of people want to do it, "I want to lose weight. I want to lose weight." But, they don't know where to start or they're: "I don't have the money." Those can definitely limit you. Money's a big factor for all of us unless we're rich, which the majority of us are not.

I think right off the bat, those are what many people run into, is not having the money and not knowing where to look or where to start.

Do people have unrealistic expectations, or unrealistic goals?

Daniel Pollaccia: It's good that you brought that up. Once I meet with someone and I talk to them, a lot of people share similar goals, "I want to lose this much weight." or "I want to get down to this size." Most of those goals in and of themselves can be realistic given enough time frame, but I literally work with clients where I train them on a Monday at noon and by Wednesday, they tell me: "I'm not losing any weight." It doesn't really work like that. Their goal is unrealistic. It'll happen, provided you do everything that you need to do but it's just not going to happen right away. You run into that.

People get discouraged off that. Like, I'm paying this money, taking the effort and I don't see any results. Results take a couple of weeks sometimes. It's not a right away thing. I put you through a workout right now, you're not going to see results in an hour. You're not going to see them tomorrow. You work out, you eat well, and you rest. Eating well and resting adequately is what gets results. It changes your body and over time it becomes a lifestyle.

Plateaus are something we get in all areas of life. Definitely in fitness, I've hit plateaus myself. What you do, sometimes you hit plateaus because you've been training hard. Your body's sore, it needs a rest. I highly recommend massage if people can afford it, it really helps recovery and injury prevention. Sometimes, with plateaus, I'll have someone back off for a week and not train. Let their body recover and then tweak the workout a little bit, make some changes, keep the basics there. I always say basics work the best. Keep the basic exercises there, change how much weight their moving, change the sets, change the reps. Then, we come back. Most of time that will do the trick. The human body adapts very quickly and making little changes when needed goes a long way. We all have our genetic limits but most of the time, when people have been hitting plateaus and they don't see the weight loss or they don't see the muscle gain, we back off and make a few adjustments and then we get right back at it. It almost always works.

How important is it for people to be able to take on the instructions that you share with them so that they can achieve their goals of getting in better shape?

Daniel Pollaccia: It's important. I pretty much talk to my clients and students the way I talk to you. I'm very casual. I'm very direct. People sometimes if they've had previous injuries or they are moving a weight that's heavier than they have moved before, sometimes they'll say "No, I don't want to do it."

I have clients who are afraid to do jumping exercises, jump rope or jump squats. You have to have faith in me that I'm not going to make you do something that's going to injure you. Some people want to just tell people they workout and some people are hard to coach. "I'm not doing that." You have to be open to try new things and have faith in your trainer.

I always tell my clients if you have faith in me, then everything will be fine because I know what I'm doing. Sometimes it scary to be physically active when you haven't been and you're sore and you hurt because you haven't used the muscles before. The soreness from training can scare people too. I've gotten texts from clients saying how sore they are and it is because they haven't been active in a very long time and their body wasn't used to it. If you have an open mind and take instruction and are willing to listen, you'll always get great results.

Share something of a case study where somebody came to you and they didn't really have that ability, or they weren't demonstrating that ability to learn and take instructions. However, you were still able to take them from point A to point B where they were successful in their fitness goals.

Daniel Pollaccia: I had a client last year and into this year, as a matter of fact. It was a referral through a friend. This person had been referred to me before and never followed through on it. So, I was hit up about training her. She expressed interest, which she had done before. We started training. She'd been a lifelong smoker. Struggled with a lot of stuff, was resistant to listen to a lot of stuff. She would often say, "Daniel, I can't do that." I make it a rule when I train you that you're forbidden to say, "I can't."

We need to be realistic. If I want you to jump up and touch a 20 foot ceiling, obviously, you can't do that. But other than that, I never want to hear the word "can't" come out of a client's mouth. She was very resistant at first. Very nice lady, but very resistant to a lot of the stuff I was teaching her, which was really simple stuff like basic push-ups.

She struggled with those push-ups. She would break down and cry, "I don't know I'm even wasting my time doing this." I got her through it and then over time, she started becoming addicted to the lifestyle after she started seeing the results and started liking the euphoria that kicks in after you workout. She eventually lost over, 30 pounds working with me.

She got a new job so she works a lot more now, but I still see her a couple of times a week, sometimes more, sometimes less, depending on her schedule but it's a real success story. I didn't know after those first couple of weeks what was going to happen with. We tracked the weight loss and everything and it's been pretty awesome actually. I'm really proud of her.

I'm just thinking, with that lady, what if for example she made money to be the obstacle, she wouldn't have been able to make that transformation, in the first place, right? At the end of the day, does the money obstacle actually turn out to be more expensive in the long run?

Daniel Pollaccia: It can be because, for personal training you need disposable income. If you're able just to pay your bills and buy food and stuff and you don't have anything left over, well, as far as personal training goes, you're not going to be able to afford it. However, even a little bit extra that you have is always worth investing because investment is not just putting money away to save.

People think money investment is real estate, Wall Street, stuff like that, but investing in your health is the most important thing. I tell people all the time. It's an investment in your health. I'm not here to take your money. I'm here to help you live longer and be able to enjoy your life. There's nothing worse than someone who's in the mid-thirties, late thirties, early forties and they have a laundry list of health problems because they don't take care of themselves.

Taking care of yourself and being in shape is a lot easier than people think it is. Some people are intrinsically motivated like myself. I don't need someone to motivate me, I can motivate myself. Other people need that extrinsic motivation where they need an outside source and I try to provide that outside source for people. People often say, "I want to look like that actress. I want to look like that actor." It's always easy to say that but taking that first step is always hard and it does come down to money, but I'm not a salesman. I don't try to sell people, I just tell them how it is and the steps that will need to be taken and we go from there.

Let's talk about some of the misconceptions out there surrounding getting into better shape and increasing your fitness level. What are some of the general misconceptions that you've come across?

Daniel Pollaccia: Misconceptions, I mean, it kind of goes back to what I was talking about earlier about realistic goals. There's a misconception that once you start working out, you see results right away. Genetics can play a role in that. I know people that barely touch weights and they're huge. Sometimes, some people after only week of working out can already see a difference. It's kind of a double answer but that's what I see a lot.

Female clients often come to me with a picture of Scarlett Johansson or someone and say, "I want to look like that." Her job is to look good all the time and she's a millionaire and she can afford to have a chef and a trainer and train whenever she wants to. A lot of people don't get that.

I think it's unrealistic, maybe societal image pressures or something but I think that is one of the most common things I come across. I want to look like that person. It's always the motivation, "I want to look like that person." I hear that probably more than anything else.

You go to the gym, you exercise and for most, they don't see muscles popping out immediately. When does it actually happen? What's actually happening with your body when you're training?

Daniel Pollaccia: When you're actually lifting weights, you're actually damaging your body. Depending on how heavy you're lifting, you're damaging it quite a bit. A lot of micro tears, occur when you're doing a heavy squat or heavy dead lift. Even when using good technique, the strain and struggle you out your body through is causing micro tears in your muscle. You're actually getting weaker while you workout. It's when you rest and you're recovering, that's when the growth takes place.

Concrete isn't strong when it's first poured, but when it is given time to rest and sit in place, then it hardens. The human body is the same. When the muscles are given time to adapt and repair, they become stronger. A lot of people forget that. That's why diet is so important.

Do you want to go do a heavy leg workout with squats and leg presses and have your legs all pumped up and barely able to walk out of the gym and then go eat garbage? No, because it's not going to optimally recover you. You need the correct carbohydrate ratios and the correct protein in you and then adequate rest. It's hard for a lot of us with our busy lives to get adequate rest but the more we're able to sleep and eat healthy, that's when the growth occurs. That's why you don't see results right away.

Would I be accurate in saying that's contrary to popular belief because even in my day, I thought the more I trained, the fitter I'm going to get and who needs sleep? I'm young, I'm fit and I only need four to five hours sleep. However, from what you're saying, that is not true, right?

Daniel Pollaccia: There are champion bodybuilders who sleep four or five hours a night, but again they're on additional substances like steroids that add in recovery.

Steroids affect testosterone and other hormones in the body and they can make recovery quicker. That's why some athletes do them so they're able to train more. For the average lay person, like us, we need that rest. We need to eat adequately.

The protein that's in foods, that helps strengthens ... It repairs all those micro tears in the muscle and then when the muscle heals, it comes back stronger. In person, I usually do a demonstration with a pencil. I break a pencil and then simulate the healing process by putting the pencil back together again. That way, they get to see what happens with their muscle.

It's really easy to demonstrate in person and makes it easy for people to see what's occurring in their bodies. Everybody's different some people recover quickly where they can workout the next day, some people take a couple of days.

Earlier on, you said you work with people who feel intimidated by the larger fitness chains. They're going to these huge studios and feel like they might look foolish, or stupid for training. Is that something of a misconception out there that you could address for us?

Daniel Pollaccia: Yes, some people do feel out if place in large and often quite busy gyms especially if it's someone who is very big and very overweight, or obese. It's very intimidating going into a place like that if you are out of shape. You're not going to wear jeans and t-shirt. You're going to wear a little bit tighter form fitting clothes to workout in and if you're a big person, with a tight shirt or tight pants on, at least for women, you feel exposed out there and you feel like people are staring at you.

You feel you look out of place and people are going to be pointing and laughing. That actually almost never happens. Someone who is out of shape and is trying to get in shape is a great thing and nothing to be balked, or laughed at.

People are very intimidated by that. I've seen it myself even one on one. I had clients that are always asking me, "Well no one else is going to come in on our session, right?" It's like, "Of course not, it's one on one." People are always intimidated by that and I get it. We're in a very image conscious society and there's so much negativity with people that are overweight. It's definitely a concern. We see it more with women than men, but I was very big at one point, too, 320 pounds. A few people used to laugh at me because I had a belly that jiggled around. People here and there would look and stare but here I am now at 240 pounds and full of muscle.

In terms of the responsibility of the trainer, what are people's' general thoughts about that? Are there any misconceptions surrounding the role of the trainer and how it affects their goals of getting into better shape and increasing their fitness levels?

Daniel Pollaccia: We have more answers than our clients would have generally, because that's why they come to us but we don't have them all. I've run into issues where people are plateauing and I've tried different things. Genetics play a huge role in anything physical. Some people are just naturally flexible and I don't have all the answers and sometimes, roadblocks happen.

We can't figure out why someone is stuck. They are not increasing their bench press or their squat and the diet's on point and the weight isn't where it should be. We just have to sit back and look at it. Sometimes, it's that some people retain more water than other people. It's all little factors and sometimes, I didn't have the answers. I seek out the answers. I don't think I know everything.

Every trainer has a specialty. Every trainer is really, really good in one area and then is lacking knowledge in others. I've come across that with people that had a shoulder injury or a knee injury so they couldn't lift their arms up above their head. I had to adjust and do upper body exercises where it didn't jeopardize that. Sometimes people think I've got all the answers and I try to always be able to answer them but I'm not always able to. At least for myself, some trainers always feel they should have an answer for their clients. It's ok if you don't know it all, none of us

There's times where people had certain conditions. I had client that had fibromyalgia and I didn't know anything about it. I looked it up and I found out exercises that we would be able to do that would not increase that issue and we were able to work around and be successful.

Let's talk about some of the unknown pitfalls about getting into better shape. Especially if someone is out there and they're thinking, I can do this on my own. Who needs a personal fitness trainer? I'm just going to step out into the gym, do this all on my own. For those people, what are some of the unknown pitfalls that they might not be aware of?

Daniel Pollaccia: There's a lot of pitfalls. It can go from anywhere from the proper attire in clothing, it can go from that all to the just not being shown how to do the exercise properly. I used to buy all the fitness magazines that show Arnold Schwarzenegger's workout. You have his workout in there. Some people don't know what the exercise is. Now, with the internet the way it is, you can look up what a preacher curl is or what a front squat is.

You can look it up and that's great, now you have a basic understanding. But it's just like any other sport or physical activity, like baseball or football or anything, there's a technique behind everything. It's not just doing the movement you see there is much more to it than that and most videos do not break that down adequately. A baseball pitcher isn't just winding up and throwing. There's a lot technique behind it. There are certain grips. The same thing in fitness.

You have Arnold's workout in front of you, okay now, you have been shown it. You've watched a video on YouTube and you might if you're a visual learner grasp the basic understanding of what they're doing but you need someone who's been there, like myself, to show you the proper way to grip the barbell, or grip the dumbbell. There's a method to it.

A lot of people would just ... They're stubborn and they think that they know what they are doing and that's when injuries happen. It's happened to me, trying to a bench press that was too heavy. I thought: "I got this. I can do this. I don't need anybody." I've walked that path so I make sure that others don't have to.

Is a having enough time to actually do the training itself an unknown pitfall?

Daniel Pollaccia: Yes. With the lives we all lead now. I'm a business owner now and me trying to find time to workout on my own even though that's my business is difficult because of the business. My students and clients have to come first. I was in college for six years, you have that factor. We have kids, wives, husbands, all that stuff. Sometimes that hour to get away is too much for some people but at the end of the day, we all have same 24 hours. It's how we use it that's different.

Most of the time, getting away for 30 minutes to an hour is more doable than people think it is and you'll reap the benefits. You know, 45 minutes three days a week. That's still an hour and a half or two hours that you're working out that wouldn't have been and your body will benefit from it.

Because like I said, you don't need as much as people think you do. You actually recover more when you're resting so getting a few sessions in a week that are 30 minutes to an hour long will do more good for people than think it will. Most people don't think they have that time but is 30 minutes really that much. I mean, we play on our phones longer than that.

Maybe there's something out there about the kind of fears that prevent the people you work from getting results. Can you share your perspective as a health and fitness expert, please?

Daniel Pollaccia: I have to address the injury thing. Injury is always the biggest fear that most have. You're moving weights and the longer you do it, you're going to be moving heavier and heavier weights and there's always a few that, "I'm going to hurt myself." That's the first thing I come across. A lot of people think … They fear that they're going to look stupid.

I touched on that, too. You know, "People are staring at me." I've seen it. They fear ridicule and they fear people staring at them for too long because they think people are laughing them. That's usually not the case. There's always some idiot out there that likes to make fun of people but I think the biggest fears that I have run across are injuries. That's legit. Then, just "I'm wasting my time.", "I look fat." People feel uncomfortable.

Obviously, people are all shapes and sizes when they're starting off. In terms of their body size, are there any fears surrounding how they look and feel about themselves when they're just starting out?

Daniel Pollaccia: For sure. With women, they fear, "I don't want to be too bulky or too muscular." I get that but the hormones that men and women produce, it's a very unlikely that a woman will ever get bulky training with me unless she's on a cycle of steroids, which I'm very against. Women always think, "I don't want to look big."

It doesn't really work that way. Everything tightens up. You get definition but you don't gain huge size. Muscle growth, you need a lot of testosterone for that. Women have some, men have a lot more, which is why we tend to be bigger on average. Guys tend to not want to be thin, they don't want to be too small. They don't want too skinny, too thin. With men, I think it's more of an ego thing, it can be a weakness. Having muscles is a sign of dominance, alpha male, and men, on average will be the ones hurting themselves in the gym by lifting too much. That rarely happens with women

When you think about the people who you work with, do some of them fear not having enough time to train on a consistent basis, is that something you come across?

Daniel Pollaccia: Definitely because time is a factor in all of our lives. The way the world is now, everything is fast, fast. Go, go, go. Consistency is key but people forget that there's a lot that they can do on own. Especially if I work with someone who's never exercised before, I have them doing a lot of basic stuff, a lot of basic body weight stuff like push-ups and squats. There's times where people, I get a text or a phone call, "I can't make it in today because of this" and I tell them, I'm like, okay, well if you have to stay at home at watch your kids or someone's sick and you have to watch him. Okay, do push-ups and squats at home. It's not my entire workout. They aren't that simple but I include a lot of simple stuff like that that anybody can do.

Even going for a brisk walk is a step in the right direction. People always forget that. They think that you have to be in this environment of treadmills and weights. That's good to be around that stuff but you don't need it to get in shape.

Missing one workout isn't going to halt your progress. It's not going to speed it up but it's not the end of the world either.

What is the ideal amount of time to be training per week?

Daniel Pollaccia: That comes down to fitness goals, what you're looking for. Most people that I work with, they're the average Joe, the average person. I tell them two to three days a week, preferably three because you get that one more session and it's that much more. Me, myself, with being a gym owner and teaching martial arts, I train every day. Not as hard one day as the other because the body can't take it but I'm active every day.

I tell people, two to three days a week, preferably three just so you get that balance. Two workouts a week is good but three adds some balance to it. That's a whole other hour of training. That's a whole other hour of raising your metabolism and keeping your body healthy and keeping it where it needs to be.

Metabolism burns calories even at rest and three workouts a week will spike that metabolism a little bit more than two so those other days that you're not working out, you're burning more calories just at rest. If they can only do two days a week, and that's all they can do, then we make it work with the two days a week.

Can you just share a little bit of your backstory and how it relates to what you do today?

Daniel Pollaccia: Sure. Yes, before I got into fitness and martial arts and stuff, I was quite obese. I was 320-325 at one point. I'm a pretty tall guy so I didn't always look that big but, you know, I started training, started doing martial arts and stuff and started losing some weight. I still had a really horrendous diet so I kind of plateaued, like we talked about.

I started researching stuff and I realized there was more that I could be doing than just martial arts. I'm doing all this stuff, which is good and I lost weight and then I started studying certification programs and I found an accredited company that certifies personal trainers.

I took a course and took a test and I got certified. Then, I started learning about diet, the proper way to workout. I've been training people since 2006, so over ten years ago. I being big like that. I have pictures. They're on my social media pages. I show people pictures of me when I was heavy and they asking me who that was and it was me. I know what it's like to be miserable. I remember not being able to sleep some nights very well because I too heavy and I had to slosh my body around because I was slow. I know all those things.

I know what it's like to be bullied and made fun of all because you're fat, because you're big, because you're overweight. Almost everything that people have dealt with or they fear, it's happened to me. You'll never get any of that with me. I understand it. I understand the mindset. That's a huge thing.

A lot of trainers, they're not bad trainers, but they've always been in shape and had a six pack and always been super thin. They know their stuff in terms of training people but they can't always relate to their clients. The guy that looks like a fitness model, that's great. He puts in a lot of work. He knows his stuff but I know what it's like to have been the polar opposite of that.

We don't see 350 pound guys on the cover of magazines usually. You see 180 pound guys that are shredded with a six pack and pecs. Most People don't understand or grasp the struggle, it's a struggle when one is out of shape, and it is a struggle to get into peak shape sometimes. I've done both. I'm pretty in shape now.

I've been on both extremes of it but society tends to lean towards one way and it makes everyone else feel like that's the norm and it's really not the norm. It's whatever makes you happy, you know ... A couple of years ago, I was working at a bar, security and I kind of decided that I wanted to go into business myself. I saved up the money. Just saved up as much as I could and last year, I opened my business. It's called Mastermind Martial Arts and Fitness.

I teach Brazilian jujitsu, which I have a black belt in. I teach kickboxing. I teach kids and then I do a lot of personal training in between those classes. It's what I do every day. I enjoy it. My school's in Victorville, California. Anybody who's ever in the area, welcome to stop by. I'd love to have you in there. It's what I do, I enjoy it. It's not work to me. I don't even look at it as a job. To me, it's just something I do. I don't look at it like as a job.

There's a lot of responsibility of course as anyone who runs a business knows, but I don't look at it like a job. I actually don't call it work. I don't let anybody else call it work either.

As part of your journey, you also got your certification, right? The NFPT?

Daniel Pollaccia: Yes, the National Federation of Professional Trainers. Yes, I've been certified under them since June 2006.

What would be your best piece of advice to somebody out there who's considering, or is even in the process of getting themselves into better shape and working on their personal fitness?

Daniel Pollaccia: Take that first step. I mean, it's always intimidating. I was intimidated. You have to start somewhere ... You don't get results without hard work and you have to take that first step. I think there's an old saying, like, a journey of a 1000 miles begins with a single step or something along those lines. It's true. You have to take that leap of faith. You have to.

I've reaped the benefits of taking that risk and here I am later. I have a successful business and I'm in really good shape. It's all because I wanted to make a change. This time of year is perfect. It's December now. A lot people on January 1, "I'm going to get in shape."

People want to because it's easy to start on the first but start today. Start right now. Many people think it is easier if you start on January 1 and people always do that but if you're serious, you'll start right now. You've just got to take that first step. What's the worst that could happen? No one can ever answer that. You're trying to improve yourself. What bad can come of it? You're trying to improve yourself.

You're not doing anything that's bad. You're doing something that's good for yourself. There's really no risk. Obviously, if you're doing the right things and take the right path to get there and don't just try to squat 400 pounds your first day, you're going to be fine.

If somebody wants to know more about you, somebody wants to get in touch with you, how would they be able to find you?

Daniel Pollaccia: They can always hit me up on my personal phone number. Area code **760-617-3016**. I always have my phone near me. You can either text or call. If I'm busy training someone, I'll always get right back to you. I'm also on social media, on Facebook. Just type in Mastermind Martial Arts and Fitness, I'll pop right up. Then, also on Instagram: www.instagram.com/mastermindmartialarts

I'm very easy to get a hold of. I always return any and all messages sent to me. Sometimes, I don't get to them right away if I'm really busy with something, but I get back to everyone. Of course, if you find yourself in Victorville, California, my school Mastermind Martial Arts and Fitness is at 12180 Ridgecrest Road, Suite 404, Victorville, California. Come in, check it out. I'd love to have anyone stop by.

Do you have any final thoughts that you'd like to share?

Daniel Pollaccia: Like I said, don't be afraid to improve yourself. There's nothing wrong with trying to be a better person especially through fitness. It will increase your life, you'll probably live longer and it enriches your life. It makes you a happier person. A lot of times, people eat bad food and they sit around and don't do anything. Food affects your mood believe it not.

There's nothing wrong with trying to improve your life and trying to enrich it and make it better. Don't let any preconceived notions you may have hold you back, because most of the time, our worst enemy is ourselves. If we can control what's between our ears, then the sky's the limit for what we can achieve.

HANNIEL PUELL

A Conversation with Hanniel Puell
Nutritionist, Strength and Conditioning
Coach of Progressive Physical Therapy, PC

Hanniel Puell, is a Nutritionist and Strength and Conditioning Coach at Progressive Physical Therapy, a private owned outpatient practice providing evidence based rehabilitation care.

During this interview, Hanniel shares educational insights about overcoming symptoms of pain, so you can return to, and sustain the kind of active lifestyle you once had.

Who's your ideal prospect Hanniel, who do you help?

Hanniel Puell: My perfect prospects are usually individuals who are suffering from pain, which limits them to begin or either continue their daily regimen. It could be an athlete who is sidelined from a knee injury, the weekend warrior who had the nagging shoulder or elbow pain, which limits their performance, or even parents who, like myself, need to keep up with their kids and not worry about their backs going out on them when they need to chase them or pick them up. Whatever the case may be, I help create a program that helps overcome their symptoms to continue and live their life pretty much carefree.

When you think about those people you help the most, what are two to three common obstacles you find that prevent them from returning to that active lifestyle that they seek?

Hanniel Puell: Sure. The first obstacle is definitely not knowing what exercises they can do. Many people ask me what is the best exercise for a bum knee or a nagging back. My answer is always, it all depends on what's happening around that affected area. For example, does the knee hurt because of a meniscus issue or is it a strain in one of the ligaments or is it a tendon issue? I mean, the same thing could go for the back. Does your lower back hurt because of this existing disc issue, did it experience some sort of trauma, or is it some sort of postural component where the pelvis can be anteriorly tilted?

Regardless of the situation, the key is to first understand what is occurring and how the injury could have taken place initially so we can create a plan that will help address that issue. It is not uncommon to see individuals continuously perform exercises they think are helpful when, in reality, it's actually doing more harm. Furthermore, individuals will train more of their non-injured areas, which creates muscular imbalances that can lead to an increase in compensational patterns, which then leads to higher risk of injury, which results in completely discontinuing their training.

As you can see, it's a chain reaction of multiple minor things that, over time, accumulate and ultimately result in a serious set-back. This leads to what I think is the second most common obstacle, being overwhelmed with various training and nutrition trends. Now, people tend to look for answers in various platforms to help whatever issues they may have. The question then becomes, well, which program do they choose?

We've been saturated with multiple forms of, what I like to call, "training camps" that people are confused on which is best. Especially if it fits well with their lifestyle and their current physical state. I mean, we have high interval training, circuit training, bodybuilding, Pilates, Yoga, athletic performance, Crossfit, Spin, boot camps. There's so many training platforms that I probably didn't mention all of them.

However, I truly believe that each one of these programs have benefits to the consumer. In the end, it really comes down to what the individual is looking for and do these training formats provide the support needed to help achieve their desired goal. I have seen people use a variations of certain training principles that are great, however, if done unstructured can become counter-intuitive and eventually leave the client looking the same or with no change.

It goes back to an example I use, which is a very common one, (of) a sprinter versus a marathon runner. Everyone wants to look like a sprinter but train like a marathon runner. The two training formats are completely different from one another. One is very strength-based with short bursts of high intensity while the other is more endurance. The body gets confused on what you're asking of it and over time hits a plateau. This is commonly where people tend to give up and then move on to the next "best thing". That could be true for nutrition. I mean, again people ask what should they eat or what's the best diet.

To be quite honest with you, I hate the word diet because diet, to me, is something that's temporary. If you are on a diet, that means, sooner or later, you're going to get off that diet. Unfortunately, diet is such a buzz word that advertisers and marketers take advantage of it and they completely dismiss the fact that nutrition is really a lifestyle.

Just like there various *"training camps"*, I like to say that there's multiple *"food camps"*. There's vegan, vegetarian, gluten-free, pescetarian, Paleo, low glycemic, organics, raw-foods. Again, all of these various ways of eating have major benefits to them and many people have been successful in losing weight on every single one of them. The question just becomes which one's best? The real question should be, which one is best for me? Which one of these style of eating can I find myself enjoying, easy for me to live by and most importantly, works best for my schedule?

We have to understand that individuals who have had success with their weight while following a particular "food camp", it's not because they're doing it temporarily to lose weight, they're doing it because they've adopted it as lifestyle. I know plenty of vegans and vegetarians who choose to eat that way because of a special cause, beliefs or religious purposes.

None of them do it for weight-loss purposes. It's not like, "Oh, I'm a vegetarian because I want to lose weight." No. They're usually vegetarian because the most common thing is, "I believe in animal rights. I don't believe in how they treat animals." Whatever their purposes are, they do it for themselves. Don't get me wrong, just because someone is vegan or vegetarian, automatically means that they look amazing or are healthy. Remember, to attain a healthy strong body is a combination of both nutrition and exercise.

People who are trying to look or feel better and have tried "all the diets" usually have one major thing in common, they never really allowed their bodies to adapt to the nutrition program and so, once again, they give up because they didn't really see results fast enough. This is the third obstacle that's really common, time and motivation. Everyone wants to see results now. It's unfortunate because we live in a time period where everything is fast. Faster internet speed, faster cars, faster routes, faster download speed, faster phones ... I mean, everything is fast.

Unfortunately our body doesn't change with these advancements. Our body adapts to our every changing environment which usually means as a nation we become more sedentary. That's why, I believe motivation is perhaps the most important tool needed to attain any goal. Now, motivation isn't something that is divinely inspired where you wake up one day and say, "Hey, I'm going to go and run a marathon." Quite the opposite. I mean, you have to have a strong enough reason on why you want to achieve that goal.

The goal itself has to inspire you to go out every day and work hard. An example I always use is, if you're a college student, you don't always want to study, or write papers, attend long lectures, prepare presentations, endure the countless sleepless nights, but the goal of earning that degree is so much more important that you endure all that hard work to obtain the diploma.

The same has to go for training and nutrition. If your goal is to lose fat, great! Why do you want to lose the fat? What is it specifically about that goal that will drive you beyond the hardship of training and nutrition? Will you make the necessary time to work towards that goal? I believe time and motivation goes hand in hand. If something is really important to you, you will always find time for it. If someone tells me or if someone says, "I don't have time to do this." Then, all they're really telling me is that goal isn't important to them at that time.

I hear plenty of excuses such as work, family, stress, restlessness, which are all legitimate. Trust me, I know all about that. Being a father of a one-year old, a husband to a wonderful wife, taking care of our two dogs, waking up at 4 a.m. to go train private clients, arrive home at noon to then go to my job in the clinic, to come home in the evening (sometimes to training even more clients), prepare dinner, spend quality time with the family and putting my son to sleep. I end up going to bed around 11:00 p.m. at night.

So needless to say I have some idea about being pressed with time but, even though I have my busy schedule, I always find time to train, to read, to write, to teach, and learn because my goal of being a health professional is more important to me than anything else. Time management, I honestly believe is essential to keep you on track and organized.

With that said then, Hanniel, bearing in mind those three obstacles that you just addressed, could you share with us an example of somebody who you have helped to overcome either one, or a combination of those?

Hanniel Puell: I do have a particular case that I have that I worked with. This person, she's a great, great individual. She actually originally started as a physical therapy patient at the clinic that I was working with, and she suffered from a back injury. The back injury sidelined her. Her goal was being able to ride her horse again. When she first arrived in the clinic she was not able to even bend over.

All she kept repeating is, "I want to go back to horseback riding. I want to go ahead and drop 10-15 pounds to allow me to do it." Keep in mind this person was overweight at that time of the injury. When she came in for back problems, her concern was if I go to a traditional gym or a program, what can or can I not do that will re-aggravate my back? Once she was done with her physical therapy, she enlisted my services, and so we started working with one another.

First off, we targeted her nutrition. It was all about what does she enjoy to eat, what doesn't she like to eat, what's her schedule, what does she find feasible for her to do. Once we knocked that down and continued on with that process, then we started focusing on her training regimen. Since I knew she had a back injury, I knew she needed stabilization, strength and endurance to be able to ride her horse.

Once we set a training program it was all work and dedication. We've been working for about a year and a half now, and I'm really happy to say that this person ... She's still with me ... She has dropped 50 pounds with the program that we've been doing and most importantly without even dieting.

Everyone that looks at her sees her coming into the clinic says, "Wow! You look amazing." All of her co-workers ask her what kind of diet is she on? What is it that she's eating? Everything she tells them is like, "I'm not on a diet." Her co-workers are amazed at her because she can go up to the candy jar at work and eat some pieces and still look amazing.

These results are attainable for everyone, we just have to spend a bit more time in understanding your nutrients rather than what they are. It's not about restricting yourself. It's like if you tell someone not to do something or not to eat something, it's only going to make you want them even more. It's human behavior. I see it even in my one-year old boy. I tell him to not touch the light bulb or open the cabinets. I move him away. What is he going to do? He's going to want to go even more.

It's all about educating ourselves. I mean, look, if you're going to go ahead and eat this, okay, let's use that to your advantage. How can we make that work for you? The same goes for training. If you want to go ahead and ride horses, great. Let's develop a program that's going to allow you to do the actions required to do.

That's why more of an individualized program tends to be better and these one-size-fits-all program can sometimes work against what you want. Quite frankly, not every movement or not every exercise is appropriate for every individual.

When you think about people who you help the most, what are some of the misconceptions they may have about overcoming symptoms, pain and returning to that active lifestyle they so desire?

Hanniel Puell: One of the misconceptions that people have is that corrective exercises or functional training is only for rehab. In all honesty, functional training could be applied in three different arenas in health and fitness. One of the greatest functional strength coaches, his name is Michael Boyle, describes function as purposeful. As a result, functional training could be purposeful training. Yes, corrective exercises is one of the aspects of physical therapy among other things.

I've been working in an outpatient PT clinic for over three years and have much respect for the therapist. I've learned so much from them in regards to the physiology, human anatomy, movement, and structure. If we're going to go ahead and look into the personal training arena, functional training could be looked upon as the new warm up.

In decades past, the old way of thinking of warming up, was jumping on a cardio equipment for 10 to 15 minutes. Then, if I'm going to go ahead and work on my back, then I will hit the lat pulldown machine and do a warmup set of lightweight to "get my body going". Once I knock that out, I'm going to go and perform my normal sets with my normal weights of my program. What we have learned over these last years in the field of functional training has led up and create a more sophisticated program that will optimize the efficiency of all of the movements. By doing so, we perform better, we reduce the risk of injury by improving the forced output and length tension relationships of the muscles. We're not only working against compensational patterns but we're not really allowing our joints to grind against one another.

Finally, in the sports performance arena, the whole goal of functional training is pretty much longevity. This could be especially true for professional athletes because this is how they earn their living. If they're injured and they're sidelined, they won't be able to produce as much.

Whether it's for a high-level athlete or a recreational athlete like the weekend warrior that I mentioned, functional training allow us to tune up our body and them keep aligned so we could continue performing. That way, we don't build up any injuries on top of one another or stack them up on top of one another and cause us to stop playing and performing. That's one misconception.

A second misconception that is common is "more is better". Whether you have an injury or you're focusing on losing weight, one thing you have to keep in mind that the body cannot recover or change without rest. Now, the idea of "the more I do the faster I will recover and see results" has to stop. Now, I'm not saying that you cannot do things every day but there's various factors that contribute to a proper program that will determine the type of training modality that you may require.

The third things that I see is a lot of people assume that paying for membership or hiring a trainer will automatically lead them to their desired goal. I hear this all the time where people say they've wasted their money on the gym or a program or a trainer because they didn't achieve their desired results. Now, if you're going to go ahead and pay for a service that is one action that is part of the journey to your desired goal.

Once again, it goes back to the motivation and is the goal strong enough for you to put in the work. I always tell clients, there's 168 hours in one week. Most people who work with a trainer, they usually see that trainer two times or three times a week, which means two or three hours in a week. What are the clients doing that remaining 165 hours in that week?

This is why I always tell them I am not the one that's going to make them lose the weight. That is their responsibility. All I do is I provide them the tools and I guide them to make sure they succeed in doing that. If they put all the responsibilities on me, they are going to be experiencing a rude awakening. If they don't take responsibility for their work or for their actions, then they're going to continue on that vicious cycle of "I'm going to try this one day, if it doesn't work, okay, let's move on to the next thing", and they'll never find the satisfaction that they're looking for.

I know you said three but there's this last misconception that really gets to me. It's most likely the most important one, it's probably my biggest pet peeve, which is people think nutrition is diet.

Now, one of the main reasons why I see majority of the people really fail in their transformation is primarily because of their nutrition. Now, it doesn't matter how hard you train, how heavy you lift or how strong you become. If your goal is to see aesthetic results, then nutrition plays a key role in that. I mean, there's a saying that says abs are made in the kitchen. It's completely true.

Unfortunately, we have a lot of people who come to us because they need to change their health and they say they tried everything and nothing works. Once again, I always tell them it's not that you failed the diet, it's the diet failed you. That's because diets are temporary, which means you cannot sustain that way of eating for the rest of your life.

If you follow, let's say, a nutrition program that says you have to avoid this or stay away from that or this food is "bad", you're already setting yourself up for failure. There's a phrase called *"food prisons"* where you only eat what has been instructed to you and nothing else. These nutritional applications can sometimes be so extreme that is can cause a negative psychological impact and jeopardizes the metabolic function of the individual.

So, what's the best nutrition program?

In order to answer that, we have to ask a few preliminary questions.

- Do you have diabetes?

- Do you have cholesterol?

- Is there a thyroid condition we should be aware of?

- Are you anemic?

- Do you suffer from celiac or Crohn's disease?

- Do you have any allergies?

- Do you cook?

As you can see, there are various factors to consider before providing a structured plan. Especially when it comes to those metabolic conditions such as the diabetes and cholesterol. In order for the body to physically change, first the body has to address those conditions so the body can function properly and begin to produce the change we desire.

However, those metabolic changes, tend to take a little bit longer than we normally have patience for. This is why I always tell people who begin a nutrition program, to look for key signs that indicate if their nutrition plan is working. Precision Nutrition has an amazing check - list that allows people to check their physical, performance, emotional/mental and appearance that is crucial for physical transformation.

Examples include: being satisfied after meals, having more energy consistently, sleeping better, feeling like you're in a better mood. If we are consistent in maintaining these levels high, then we start seeing long term results in fat loss, if that's the goal, or recovery. Nutrition, is a huge component for both recovery and weight loss. I'm currently writing a book right now specifically on that topic and clear the message on nutrition once and for all.

For those people who are experiencing pain and wanting to overcome the symptoms, so that they can return to that active lifestyle that you help them to achieve, what are one or two unknown pitfalls that they might not be aware of?

Hanniel Puell: The first pitfall is definitely the one-size-fits-all approach for training and nutrition. There is absolutely no two individuals out there that are the same. I mean, we all have different work schedules, different health concerns, different lifestyles, different goals, and different nutrition preferences. Depending on the type of program, I mean, those one-size-fit-all may not work for you or, worse, could cause an injury to you.

It really comes down to finding something that you know is realistic for you. Personally, I can't sustain a vegetarian lifestyle so I'm not going to follow one. I know I've got a knee issue so I'm not going to do plyometric or high-interval training at this moment to prevent further injury.

I'll try corrective exercise and include other modalities that will help me in achieve my goals. I mean, there's so many platforms for you to choose but please do not choose one just because you want to see results fast. All that does is set yourself up for failure and possibly lead to injury because you may be overdoing yourself.

You want to make sure you understand your physiology, understand what your preferences are, what your schedule is so then, that way, you could go ahead and set yourself up for success. That's pitfall number one. Pitfall number two is the lack of performing Self-Myofascial Release or foam rolling, mobilization, and flexibility within their program.

Every day I see injuries caused by overuse or muscular imbalance that could completely be eliminated, or prevented if people had more mobility or flexibility. Unfortunately, these are not, I guess you could say, exciting enough or sexy enough to get the consumer ready to jump on that. To tell them, "Hey, you should do foam rolling because you're going to look great." It's hard to sell.

One of the things you have to understand is foam rolling, mobility and flexibility allows the muscles to recover quicker. It allows your joints to move in the range of motion that you need so they could perform the exercises you want.

Flexibility is also important because it helps create symmetry and balance in your muscles. I always tell people, "If you want to see your abs and you're constantly crunching and you're doing sit-ups, in order for you to see your abs, you have to move in the opposite direction. You have to stretch those ab muscles. Make the tendons of the ab muscles really contract and seal, that way you could see them on top of your proper nutrition.

That's the second unknown pitfall. I wish there was more education or more awareness of the importance of those three modalities. Then, probably the most important pitfall is patience. Everyone wants to see everything fast. Being an active person, I completely understand the frustration of nursing an injury especially if you can't perform your daily activities or exercises that you do on a normal basis because you have to wait for the healing process.

You have to allow the body to do what it needs to do but, because you're impatient, some people tend to just throw out the recommendations needed for specific area and just say, "You know what? I need to do what I got to do. I'm going to go ahead. Even if I have a shoulder injury, I'm still going to go ahead and lift because I can't stop training.

Those people who are impatient tend to have injuries for a longer period of time and never really recover. In all honesty, if you want to continue training and you have some sort of injury, you can always ask your health professional.

- What am I still capable of doing?

- Do I have any limitations?

- If I do certain things, can I do this extreme?

- How far can I push it without contributing to my issue?

99% of the time, there are always alternatives to different programs to allow you to continue your training, your weight loss, or whatever it is that you're looking for. It's all about just implementing different strategies for different scenarios.

What are two or three of the most common fears about even attempting to overcome the painful symptoms they experience on a day-to-day basis, Hanniel?

Hanniel Puell: The most common fear that I'm seeing, really, is pain. A lot of people who go through recovery or want to go back, especially rehabbing and pain injury, they confuse discomfort with pain. Their commitment and adherence to the program completely get shot because they feel like, "Oh, if it's hurting, I'm re-injuring myself and, therefore, I got to stop because I'm going to limit myself."

Quite the opposite. I always tell people, discomfort, it's to a point where, okay, I can keep on going but pain is truly a stabbing, sharp sensation like, "Oh, I got to ease up on it." You always want to go to the point of discomfort but never in pain because that's going to allow you to actually regain the range of motion, which is just as important as building up the strength or whichever area we are treating.

Believe me, I've seen this, and it's not surprising but there are individuals who have really low pain thresholds, where even the slightest discomfort, not even pain but discomfort, will prevent them from even moving or progressing forward and then they stop.

They're like, "No. I can't do it. It hurts. It causes pain." They don't see responsibility for their rehabbing or their training and then they just leave. They said, "It's going to do me more harm." Us, as professionals understanding what we're doing, we're never going to jeopardize or put anyone at risk especially when it comes to your health. We understand that. I understand that.

I'm always going to be able to allow every one of my patients and clients to reach success but, in order for us to do that, we have to put the body through uncomfortable situations and movements so that we could go ahead and progress. I always tell people fear is something that we need because every time you have fear, that means behind that fear is the goal or the person that you want to be. If you do not have that fear, then it's hard for us to move on forward and know that we're doing something right. That's pretty much the first commitment and adherence to the program.

The second thing that I've seen is people say that they know what they need to do. This can counter fear or everything, can go through for any professional because there's plenty of times where people who go up to them and tell them, "You know what? I saw a video on YouTube, or I saw something online and read up on it and it says I should do this, I should do that. I know what I need to do." In my mind, and I always go back to, *"Well, if you do know what you're doing, why are you sitting across from me on this table and why are we having this conversation?"*

There's always a reason why I'm speaking to somebody or someone comes to me. It's either because something is not going correctly or there's a misunderstanding somewhere in what you're trying to accomplish. It goes back to that simple case of knowledge versus application. I mean, you may know what you need to do but sometimes you just need somebody to hold you accountable on actually doing what you need to do. To be quite honest with you, I honestly don't believe that any of us really, all of us or any of us, know everything really.

I mean, I've been doing this for 10 years and I'm still learning. I'm still constantly reading and following up and following trends because I believe the more we learn, the better we could help those who are seeking our advice to try to improve our health and condition and our training, and especially all the epidemics that we're seeing in regards to obesity now going to childhood obesity. It's not something that we're pretty much done with. Learning is a constant thing even if you're in your 70s, 80s, 90s, you're always learning.

To finish off, the third fear is pretty much being disappointed and not seeing aesthetic results. Now, when I say this, I'm not trying to repeat myself in terms of quick enough. The fear that I'm talking about in terms of not seeing the results quick enough is more of a deeper emotional and psychological component.

Aside from the patients, it's not uncommon to see people to start to feel depressed or feel helpless or hopeless or feel they cannot achieve what they wanted to do. That impact becomes another obstacle as a professional that we have to work with because, not only do we have to focus more on the physical component, now we have to focus on emotional, psychological component.

That, in itself, is a challenge. If you understand the human psychology and physiology, emotions, and hormones play a huge part in your body and how it looks. Just look how bad stress affects the body negatively and how the body gains weight and lack of sleep? It's just evident with all of that.

That's why I believe, as professionals, we have to go ahead and educate them and have the patience and take the time and tell them, "This is what's occurring. These are the steps that we should take. These are the small goals that we should look for. These are the progress points that we should look for. Once we get that, then and only then can we move forward and achieve the long-term results that you're looking for."

Why would the people who suffer from pain and want to return to their previous active lifestyles?

Hanniel Puell: Everyone wants to change something or everyone wants to improve something about themselves in one way or another, whether it's to regain that spark from the significant other or build their self-esteem, compete at a high level, or even regain control of their lives.

Everyone wants to change something about themselves. After many failed attempts, they feel stuck and so they go ahead and seek my help. This is why I consider myself more of a coach rather than a trainer because I help guide and structure a program that will lead to success. For the most part, my tools are very simple. However, just because it's simple doesn't mean it's easy.

Do you really enjoy what you do?

Hanniel Puell: Absolutely. I love it to the point where I stay up pretty late in reading and understanding what I do because I've personally gone through this experience and I've never really understood what my meaning in life was.

Once I started helping people change in the way that I do, educate them because

I come from a family line of teachers and educators. Once I started to do things my way by helping people to change their habits and achieve the things they once believed to be impossible, once I saw their smiling faces, well, it changed me too. Now, I wake up every day feeling like I have a responsibility to help.

Could you just go into a little bit about your backstory and how it relates to what you do today?

Hanniel Puell: First off, I'm a strong, strong believer in functional training programs, which pretty much means, movement in all planes and motion to create symmetry and balance between the skeletal and muscular system.

That is why I like to say if you want to train like an athlete and not in the sense of at high demands, it's really tough going. Better to move the body in motions which allow the muscle groups to work in unison. I always feel that nutrition is a huge aspect and an important component that helps achieve any physical and nutritional preferences and lifestyle that you have.

Now, as for myself, years ago, I was an active soccer player and I was competing in elite level. Unfortunately, I suffered a collapsed lung, which ended my season. Soon after, I had to undergo surgery which, like I said, ended my season but it left me with a tube hanging out on the right side of my rib. Now, doctors warned me and said returning to soccer would inevitably reproduce my injury, perhaps soccer was done and over for me, and, to be quite honest with you, I was not ready to give up on my dream and I was most definitely not going to be told what I can or cannot do.

That's why I define my goal. It ignited my motivation. I trained hard. A year later, I came back to my team and I earned the All League MVP. From then on, I vowed I'm going to continue studying conditioning and performance, and I'm going to continue improving so then I can go ahead and help other people. As life would have it, I experienced a very strong loss in my family, which made things very difficult for me. I could honestly say that I went in extreme depression and I gained massive amount of weight. It wasn't until a few months later that I decided that it's time for me to move on with my life and regain control.

I started hitting the gym and within a few months, I started seeing improvements in my body but it wasn't the type of improvements that I was used to seeing. For some reason, it was a lot harder for me to lose my body fat now or at that period than it was before my lung injury. Then, it was then when I decided to major in nutrition. I became a certified trainer.

For the most part, I read that the answers for fat loss was all about calories in versus calories out. I read everything I could get my hands that would show me what to eat and how much I should eat. I tried limiting my portions, weighing food, counting calories, eating "healthy foods", avoiding those "bad foods". I started training daily but nothing much really changed. I hit a major plateau. Soon after weeks of doing one or many of those strict regimens and diet exercise programs, my life would get interrupted with school work, family, and I would eventually fall off the wagon. Needless to say, I was feeling frustrated and I figured there had to be a better way.

I was just starting my career as a nutritionist and so I started seeking for a way where you can lose weight and keep it off without going on ridiculous, restrictive diets, long hours dedicated to the gym. I did my research and I found that another nutrition expert, rejected the diet approach and focused on something much more simple and effective. Furthermore, the fitness industry has been advancing with much more sophisticated and proven training protocols that challenge a lot of what are the more commercial claims that have failed me, personally, countless times.

One of my biggest obstacles was that I did not define the type of training that I want to adapt. I spent years training like a bodybuilder one week, and then a physique model the next week, then a little bit of endurance athlete in between to try to polish my athletic conditioning. My body was confused.

I was doing all these different things that I would see in magazines and my body's like, "Well, which is it?" Of course, in my mind, I'm like, "What's going on?," but my body's pretty much shutting down because it doesn't know what you're asking of it.

My energy system changed especially when it came to aerobic training. Because of my collapsed lung, it was harder for me to do a long distance running a lot more so I had to focus more on the anaerobic type of training and I had to change the things. As a result, I spent a decade experimenting, testing, developing my own approach for long-term health and performance and I was successful with what I came up with.

Now, utilizing the research that I've learned from various professionals, I adopted my own approach, which finally allowed the fat to come off and I've gained the body I've always wanted. I systemized my strategy to help my clients and, together, we've seen major improvements in their health and performance.

What would be your best piece of advice to someone who is considering taking their quality of life into their own hands and doing what's necessary to beat pain, overcome their symptoms, and return to the kind of active lifestyle they once enjoyed?

Hanniel Puell: One of my best pieces of advice would be, first off, define their goal and commit to them because without a strong enough goal, the steps required to achieve that goal would feel too complicated and, eventually, will fall off.

Second, once they commit to that goal, they must commit to a program that best suits them. They have to accept that body transformation is a process and it is not achieved overnight, that they cannot lose 20 years of bad habits in 20 days.

Finally, if you feel stuck or fearful of doing a program because of risk of injury, just seek out help. Ask. Trainers, we should be looked upon as educators. We can help design programs to their specific needs.

Now, with that said though, just because a trainer is certified doesn't automatically mean that they are qualified. Make sure to do your research before you invest with a trainer and, most importantly, make sure the training style best suits with each one of your personalities and make sure it goes hand in hand because, after all, it really comes down to communication and comfort when it comes to that.

Hanniel, if someone feels you're the right person that they want to get in touch with, how can they connect with you?

Hanniel Puell: If someone really wants to go ahead and contact me either because they have pain issues, for fitness, performance, and nutrition, they could find me on my LinkedIn. By going to linkedin.com, typing in my name and sending me a connection request, or they could go ahead and email me at hpcoach@hotmail.com.

Any final thoughts before we go, Hanniel?

Hanniel Puell: Yes. My work philosophy revolves around a quote that goes, "Give a man a fish, and you feed him for a day. Teach a man to fish, and you feed him for a lifetime."

Now, I tell my clients all the time that my goal is not to keep them. My goal is to teach and educate them in understanding their human physiology and their nutrition so that one day, they have the confidence to do things on their own. Now, the fact that I have people staying with me for years is solely because they enjoy training with me.

You're not going to hear a lot of trainers say this but I get excited, in all honesty, when I hear a client say to me that they're going to continue training on their own because they feel they've learned everything that they needed to from the program. As a professional, that makes me feel accomplished. I satisfied my responsibility.

Whenever you work with a professional, make sure you learn. Ask plenty of questions. Apply the knowledge whenever possible because, after all, it's all about you, the client, regaining control of your health and not depending on anybody else but yourself.

MIKE CAULO

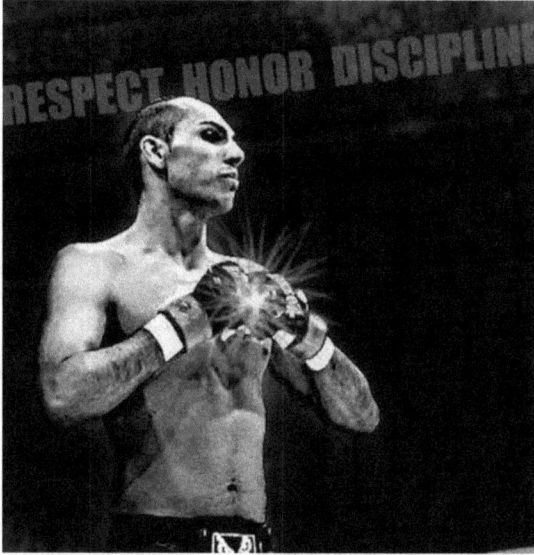

A Conversation with Michael Caulo, Certified Master Trainer, The Life of a Fighter Ltd.

For the past 5 years, Michael Caulo, Certified Master Trainer and owner of The Life of a Fighter Ltd. has been helping his clients to create a healthy lifestyle, so they can perform and feel at their best.

He holds an Associate's Degree from the International Sports Science Association, a Bachelor's Degree from Stony Brook University in Interdisciplinary Studies, as well as Certifications such as, Fitness Nutritionist, Exercise Therapist, Senior Fitness, Youth Fitness and Strength and Conditioning Specialist.

During this conversation, Michael talks shares some fascinating insights into how he's helping people to get closer to their goals of an optimally designed lifestyle.

Who's your ideal prospect Hanniel, who do you help?

Mike Caulo: The name of our company is Life of a Fighter, and I really tried to play off of that because I believe we want to help who we call fighters and that kind of carries over to everybody because everyone's fighting for something.

The biggest thing we look for and who we want to help is someone who's striving to make their lives better. Anyone that wants to progress and improve their lives, their quality of life, but really specifically, with the health optimization side of it, so, obviously we're not going to look for someone that had absolutely no interest in, let's say, maybe eating a little bit better, moving a little bit more or making any kind of change in that side of it, but we do want someone that is looking to optimize their lives.

So, when you think about those people you describe as fighters, what are two to three common obstacles you find that prevent them from creating a lifestyle for optimal health and performance?

Mike Caulo: Yes, that's a great question. It happens a lot because the first thing, I think, the biggest thing that we face is really having them be honest with themselves and being honest when they do decide to start training or working with a coach or a professional. Being honest with us and then, also like I said, being honest with themselves and being aware of their own bodies and being aware of, like you said, their own pitfalls and being aware of, also, their own strengths. Knowing what they're good at but also knowing where they may need some work as well.

So, that's the first one, then we have New Year's resolution time, being patient and being able to not just say "I'm going to go for two weeks, I'm going to work really hard and I want to lose 20 pounds". That's not how it's going to work, that's not how our body responds.

I've never seen anyone, never, not even one client, not one case, that in two weeks has hit their goal and then they're able to stop and then just go back to an old lifestyle, it's really about being patient with us, the program and themselves to let that change happen and to let progress happen over time. And then, to follow up with that, being patient is one part of it but then also being consistent with it as well, by making it a lifestyle and allowing it to make those changes and moving forward.

Please share an example of somebody who you've helped overcome one of those three obstacles.

Mike Caulo: I have a perfect client in mind, especially for being honest and aware because this client, again, without naming names, I ran into them in the gym, in one of the gyms that, you know, I work out of and this is the kind of person that was in fitness their whole lives. So growing up, they grew up in a gym, they had that environment but at some point this individual went into the corporate America world. They were just constantly working for corporations, traveling, they had a family, they end up having kids and at some point, they really weren't being honest with themselves and I don't think they were being aware of what was happening in the sense that they weren't training the same, they weren't living that same lifestyle and they let the traveling, the stress, the obligations, the family, all of those things, take over their life and all of a sudden gained 50 pounds.

When I say all of a sudden, they didn't obviously all of a sudden gain 50 pounds, but in their mind they woke up one day and they're like "I'm 50 pounds heavier, where did this come from?" It happened over years but of course because, again, they weren't, going back to this idea of, being honest and aware with themselves and looking in the mirror and going "I'm not living this lifestyle" and obviously the weight's going up, it's adding on and then all of a sudden, you look in the mirror and you're 50 pounds heavier.

So, that was one aspect of the being honest and aware aspect, then I have another client, for getting patient and the idea of wanting to a) get results now, you absolutely have to balance that idea but also being able to look at what's the long term picture.

So, and this is a younger client of ours who overcame that first obstacle of being aware and honest with himself. He lost the initial weight but now, he's a 16 year old kid and, just like every 16 year old guy that's grown up, they want to be jacked, they want to impress girls, and they want it all in a very short period of time. To help, we develop programs with him and set specific goals.

Another important point is to understand is you can go into a great program and a plan, but, again, part of that plan has to be an end destination. You have to have something you're working towards and we do it in two to four week measurements and then we have a 12 week assessment at the end that we're looking towards. The way we broke it down is we wanted to lose body fat percentage while maintaining muscle mass so that we don't lose too much and fall too far behind.

Anyways, I'm going off on a tangent, but the whole take away from this was, in the first two weeks he went down a half a percent of body fat, which is really great, he was on track. However, in his mind it wasn't enough. He'd say, "Oh well, you know, I'm going to have to train extra and I'm going to have to do more, and eat less." A

Then he starts to make his own adjustments because he wasn't being patient, he wasn't staying with the program. Over the next two weeks, his body fat percent actually increased because he over-trained. He ended up gaining a little bit of fat and was losing a little bit of muscle so that threw his numbers off and once he saw that, he kind of realized, "Okay, I see what you mean by being patient, I'm seeing that my body's not responding the way we want it to," and that kind of goes back, even tying in with the third obstacle, being consistent.

It's be patient with the plan but then consistently following the plan that we had set for him and then at the end of those 12 weeks, he did see a nice drop in his body fat percent, meaning a drop in his body fat percentage, and now, even to this day, we've been able to, a year later, get his body fat to drop under 10% body fat and continue to improve his body composition. He's got the abs he's wanted and all the benefits that come with that from psychological a stand point, even with girls and all the fun stuff athletically, and it kind of just snowballs from there.

What are two to three popular misconceptions that they may have about attaining an optimal lifestyle for health and performance?

Mike Caulo: The misconception is such a huge aspect of maintaining a lifestyle because there's a lot of times you'll have [inaudible 00:06:03] misconceptions that will be a short term, okay, maybe it can work, but long term it's just not going to work and that's where we've got to break them down and the biggest one, I think, is food can't be enjoyable. People have this conception, "Oh, I have to go on a diet", especially when it comes to New Year's resolutions, or its right before the summer, the season change.

People want to have this, kind of, last minute and they keep pushing it off and there's a lot of different psychological reasons for that as well but I think one of the bigger ones is because they're dreading, they have a negative association with changing their lifestyle habits, especially when it comes to food and that's because they just assume, well, the food's not going to taste good, I'm going to have to sacrifice something there and I don't want to do that.

So, I think that's the biggest one that we can break down for everyone. You can still enjoy your food and the other side of it, is that you don't have to starve yourself. So, a lot of times we'll look at, everyone's thinking "Okay, I've got to cut my calories in half" or "I've got to eliminate carbohydrates, or maybe I should just eliminate ...", there's a certain type of food they might look for to just completely eliminate and take out, or is it the idea of going back to even a calorie deficit of well, do I only eat twice a day, do I eat five times a day, 20 times a day. Where's that, kind of, middle ground, and that's another side of it. Enjoy your food. I, kind of, go back to that because that's the main principle.

What do you enjoy first and then we build off of it because if I come to you, sir, and I say, "You know what, we're going to take what you're doing right now with your lifestyle and we're going to completely change everything, from head to toe, we're going to flip you on your head and nothing's going to be the same.

"I would put all of my money that you're going to fail, not because I'm doubting you, but because of what the psychology and the habits say about us as people. It's just not going to work.

So I think that's a really big misconception. The other one that we're going to go into... which is really important, is that some exercises are for athletes only. I hear a lot of people question me when I give them, and even a lot of our coaches that we work with, give exercises, for example, let's say, a deadlift, which is a heavier movement, or certain types of squats.

Or maybe even a bench press. They think that, well, I'm not trying to play football, I'm not trying to play any athletic kind of endeavor, why should I be doing that movement? Isn't it going to hurt my knees? Things like that, but, truly, these movements should be the staple of almost everybody's programming, depending on, obviously, different injuries, different goals, but there are certain staples that almost should be in everything, because they're just so beneficial for our bodies.

And then the last misconception I think that I really want to mention is ... You can outwork a poor diet. People think, again, going back to, it kind of relates, tying into food can't be enjoyable. People want to enjoy this food they eat, well, I'll just do an extra mile or I'll do an extra hour on this StairMaster or I'll just add a little extra and sometimes it can work like that but a lot of times, it's not as simple as I'm going to outwork the poor food choices that I made.

There's other factors to it, right, if we time it right, yeah, maybe we can, but a lot of times it's not going to work ... Let's take, for example, one cookie might be a mile and a half on the treadmill, so just think about what a pizza slice is going to be. That's going to be at least three to four miles, so when you add it up, like, well, did I have five slices of pizza, so that means, okay, five slices, that means I have to run 20 miles.

You kind of see it can, exponentially grow and you start having larger servings of food ... This is where serious damage can be done to our progress. But if you can make better choices knowing the risk, then I believe you are going to make huge strides right there.

What are one or two unknown pitfalls that they may not be aware of when attempting to reach an optimal lifestyle for health and performance?

Mike Caulo: Yeah, this is one of my favorite questions because it is not only looking at the physical, but this is where we can kind of dive into some of the psychological aspects because I think the bigger pitfalls we're going to face can be from a psychological and sociological standpoint.

What I mean by that is, look at your social circle, and look at the environment you're in, and the people you surround yourself with.

Are they supportive of your goals?

And what I mean by that is not just giving you a high five and a slap on the back, but are they eating cookies in front of you when, let's say, you're eating something else. Now, let's say you have a nice meal, you're still eating a good salad or you're having a good ratio ... Let's say, some chicken with some whole wheat pasta and veggies on it ... Whatever it is that you're eating, but you may also want a cookie and you have your friend, your brother, your ... Whoever, your mom, your significant other and they're eating a cookie in front of you.

Now, they may say they're supporting you but to me, their actions are saying they're really not, unless you say, listen, I'm at a point where I have such happiness and discipline with what I'm doing and control where I'm not even going to be tempted, that's completely fine but realistically, are they being supportive with their actions not just their words and I think that's the biggest pitfall that I see with clients is, it's even.

A lot of times it's the significant other that may not be on the same game plan or may not be on the same page as far as their health and fitness and I'll have one person that will want to do it and the other person's like, kind of, on the fence or they're really not as interested and they end up wanting to go out, get drinks, do other things that are going to be just not where the client is ready to be yet because of all the things we're trying to reconstruct or just, kind of, develop and change. So, that's a really big one.

And the other one that I see that, this one kind of goes back to the medical side of things, is sometimes a client will just have an underlying health issue that, either themselves, they tried to kind of self-medicate or that their doctor is addressing with medication first and not properly implementing a good nutrition and training plan.

Again not to say certain conditions won't be solved with medication or that shouldn't have medication, that's a hundred percent not the case but there's a lot of preventative measures we can make and complementary measures we can make with food and training and a good fitness plan that will help that they need to be able to properly understand and that's what we try and do now with implementing, even, certain blood work and assessments with health we can look at, are you just vitamin deficient and that may explain why you're feeling nauseous or why your hormones might even be off, an x, y and Z type of situation. This is where we specialize as a company, we integrate multiple strategies to find the best solution for the client.

When you're thinking about these people who you describe in your own words as fighters, these people who have this burning desire, this inner spirit to really make a change and optimize their lifestyle for maximum health and performance, what are some of the most common fears that actually hold them back?

Mike Caulo: Yeah, this one I think gets really interesting. The first ones, I think everyone's really afraid of at first putting in the work and what if they fail? In the back of their mind, a lot of people are going to think, well, what if I do all this and it doesn't work, what if I can't achieve my goal?

That's a very scary reality for people to face and I think it's not just with what I see in health and fitness but even what I've seen as an entrepreneur, what I've seen as an individual and I think what we've all seen at some point is that you have to be able to understand that sometimes in life you're going to fail and that's actually a beneficial thing, and it can be good, but getting the client to initially accept that they shouldn't be scared of the failure and if they trust the program, they communicate with us and they're patient and they're consistent and they're being honest with themselves and with us, that fear is really unnecessary and it's just something that they're going to overcome very quickly.

Another one that I see, and this is one of my favorite quotes that I see a lot of athletes use and, just, a lot of successful individuals is, "Our deepest fear is not that we are inadequate, our deepest fear is that we are powerful beyond measure."

That reaching full potential and knowing what that is, it can be easier to think what if, and create hypotheticals as opposed to finding out with a lifelong pursuit. So, basically, kind of, summarizing the initial quote and the explanation after it is, once we get over that initial fear of, like, okay, failing, now the fear of what about the success, what about actually obtaining that goal and everything that comes along with it, it can actually scare a lot of people because of all the things associated with it.

I think that's kind of an exciting idea. Once we can get the client or whoever to understand that first, trust us, we'll get you there and then be okay with getting your goals. This goes back to being honest and being aware, are you really okay with achieving that goal in the back of your mind/

You then think what about a) my significant other, people around you, all these other factors that may come in, and then b) what about a lifestyle that goes with it, are you really embracing that, are you ready for it? Because you should be, and you deserve it. Everyone deserves to be at their best, it's just after, maybe, years of being in a certain spot or just being comfortable or other environmental factors, things can change.

And then the last one I would like to mention, this one's a little bit more specific for women but, the idea that bulking is going to happen when we lift weights. And they have a lot of fear of, well I don't want to be bulky, I don't want to look too big and I'm not saying that it's impossible, and I'm not saying that it's not even an outcome of weight training but, not just for women but for anyone, to actually get bulky when they lift weights, it has to be an effort.

You actually have to plan for it, unless, you're genetically prone to putting on a lot of muscle mass, then high fives to you and then we can have a really easy time of accommodating how to make that into your goals, but, especially for women, the fear of bulking up and getting too big, it would take such a drastic effort of increasing calories and training a certain way that it's very uncommon for that to happen unless, a) your coach or your trainer has no idea what to do and you're just guessing on your own or b) again, you're genetically predisposed to that and then we make such adjustments, and then you're going to be lean or get your goal, or whatever you want to get to, we can get you there.

When I was young, super fit, and growing up in the UK, I used to play a lot of football, or as you guys in the States call it, Soccer, at a very high level. I had the kind of body that used to change rapidly and whenever I did training, muscles were just popping out everywhere within days. I used to be afraid of pushing myself too much because I didn't want to get bulky, so I find it fascinating that you're speaking about women getting bulky. Have you ever had that experience of guys who also have that fear of getting too bulky for their particular sport or lifestyle?

Mike Caulo: Yeah, that's a great point. What you're talking about, especially soccer athletes, I've had soccer athletes that we've had to look at that, as well as fighters, mixed martial artists, kickboxers, boxers, even grapplers and wrestlers. I work with those as well, and we have to be cautious of weight and their muscle to fat percentage and ratio, how much their total weight is.

I think the important thing is keeping a balance of how much muscle mass we're putting on. If you're one of those people who are naturally going to put on muscle, that's great. That means we won't have to put you through that much weight training to keep you at a pretty high quality muscle mass to fat ratio, and keep you lean. However, what we'll focus on is more explosive, neurological firing. When you add up the total amount of running you're doing in a given game in soccer, you're running miles.

You're not consecutively running them, you're going to have intervals, and at some points you might not even be running at all, you might be just, kind of, standing, waiting for the play to happen and then you're going to lightly jog, then you might have to sprint when the action's picking up. Through the course of the game, there are intervals, highs and lows, and that's what we would focus on.

There are very few endurance athletes that want a low intensity, slow twitch endurance training, such as marathon runners and triathletes. Even then, we're still going to work in some intervals so almost everyone, from an athletics standpoint will benefit from fast twitch muscle firing.

That's where we can keep the muscle tissue from growing or bulking too much, because we're going to control the mass with the intensity.

I'd also look at what are you are eating. When you were playing football, I'm assuming you're probably ate a good amount because of high levels of intensity and lots of training. Whether it's good or bad, even if it's the best quality food, if you were eating at a high caloric intake, too much for your body to process, you're would have to have sored it somewhere, whether it's fat or muscle, so that's something we would have looked at as well.

Sounds like an obvious question, but why would anybody want to gain optimal health and performance?

Mike Caulo: I think it's such an important question to ask because this is the biggest thing that I think that I would really like to see with our education system from a younger age. I would like to see health classes really emphasizing why good health is so important. What is it doing? Does it actually have an effect on me, not just to know, all right, I know some diseases, I know kind of how my body's laid out, but teaching how does the brain and the body work together, that's the biggest thing for optimal health and just an optimal lifestyle, quality of life. What I look at, regardless of if you're an athlete, regardless if you're just a corporate professional, you're a stay at home mom, you're a student, whatever you are, a lot of times we'll have our brain and we'll think it's separate than our body.

That's how they're meant to operate, your brain, your body are meant to operate 100% together and what we want to do is have the communication between, whether it's your stomach when you're getting hungry, it's communicating to your brain, which is triggering the hormonal response and a chemical response, which is what's causing an excessive hunger for you to overeat and then all the chain reactions that happen from there, or from an actual physiological standpoint of movement.

From the kinesiology standpoint of it, if you're feeling back pain, if you're feeling aches and pains, that can also just be from stemming from the gut and the food that you're eating.

So, for me, it's beneficial to gain that optimal health and performance, to understand your body, to have that brain body connection and to just feel better overall. If I could give you a pill, instead of exercise and training, I guarantee you everyone would take it. So some of the reasons why someone would want to gain optimal health and performance could be to lower risk of heart disease, lower risk of cancer, live a longer life, and improve quality of life.

As long as you're be able to move more, you're going to be in less pain. You're going to be able to extend the quality of your life not only from in your 40's and 50's but throughout your 60's, 70's and even your 80's. The percentages of you moving more go up drastically.

Some of my certifications are for the elderly. 80% of elderly people over 65 will not walk unassisted again after they fall. Meaning, if you fall and let's say you break an arm, hip, leg, or any other kind of injury after 65, you have an 80% chance of not being ale to walk unassisted again. You're going to need a cane, walker, or wheelchair. So, weight training, just by itself, even without all the beneficial nutrition, will help impact that. So, to me, the optimal health is again the brain, body connection but also the best quality of life you can have until the day you leave this world, or pass on.

So, the obvious question was obviously a really important question to ask, just listening to that list of benefits that you shared with us there, Mike.

Mike Caulo: That's the biggest thing, I told you all the benefits you get from that, if it was in a pill, wouldn't you take that pill?

Oh, yesterday!

Mike Caulo: Exactly, because we're in that idea of, like, well, okay, a medication for this, a medication for that, trust me, there's so many benefits to having that quality of lifestyle, it's better than any pill you could really take.

So, with that said, could you share a little bit about your backstory and how it relates to what you do today?

Mike Caulo: I always tell everybody this, just to understand more about my perspective and where I am coming from.. I was always chubby as a baby, a child, an adolescent up until I was 16 years old, I always had extra weight on myself and, so I can relate to the individual that may not feel a hundred percent comfortable in their own skin, let's say, because of an overweight factor and throughout that, you know, I always played sports, I played baseball throughout my entire life, my family was active, my brother played baseball, he's younger than me, so we were always playing together.

But on the other side of it, I was active, I just loved food. I grew up Italian and German and lots of home cooked foods, lots of pasta, lots of heavy goulash and soups and, just, cream sauces, so I was always eating, so even though I was outside playing and all that fun stuff, I was always coming in, and again, you can't outwork a poor diet. I'm the perfect example of that. I would have all this activity but I would just out eat myself and not really allow myself to get the results from all my activity. I didn't know any better, I was a kid, obviously, and even for your younger ages, you don't really know until other factors come up.

Also, when I was younger, around seven or eight, I started martial arts, you know, I had anger problems, also my parents were kind of, from a younger age, even five and six, all the way up until I was 16, they were breaking up, getting back together, and I have amazing family, amazing parents, they just weren't good for each other and it's one of those situations where that happens, that's life, but, as a young kid, when your environments changing like that, it's stressful.

There are a lot of factors, I had anger and found martial arts as another outlet (besides baseball), to release that energy because in baseball, as much as I loved it, and it was fun, you just can't get the same outlet. In martial arts, you get to hit things especially since I was doing TaeKwonDo, I got to kick and learn discipline and structure which I think is very important.

So, that kind of started the younger aspects of getting into my martial arts journey and then as I grew, I kind of started my interest in martial arts but also, kind of, into the fitness style as well and realizing there's a lifestyle factor to it.

I was very fortunate that my grandfather, he would also watch a lot of martial arts movies or different shows, like Chuck Norris and Bruce Lee and he saw Highlander, and it had all these cool martial arts things, so I really looked up to that.

It's ironic, I never knew I'd be a fighter in another part of my life but it's funny how it comes full circle but because of, going back to the baseball side of it, I found a strength coach when I was 14, because I wanted to improve my baseball, like a lot of younger kids coming up and you're going to say competitive, you're going to have to invest in what you're doing.

You can't just take all the off season off and not really dive into improving your skills, so that's what I sought to do with this strength coach, John Furia at Xceleration Strength Training, that was right by my house in Deer Park on Long Island and John has literally had one of the biggest impacts of my life. He was a mentor of mine, he's a friend to this day, he's still currently a mentor, I still work with him and talk with him and he had such an impact in my life. I'm very grateful for him and for all the things that he's been able to do.

When I was about 15, I was going onto the varsity team and I ended up getting cut and my coach was ... I also respect my baseball coach, Mr Migliozzi he was very honest, too. He's not going to, kind of, beat around the bush. He told me, "Look, listen, you're just too slow, I can't have you on the team". His style of baseball was fast, you've got to be able to run, it's like, in soccer, if you're not able to move, right, it's just not going to work-

So, his style was, he wants to steal bases, be aggressive and I couldn't fit into that game plan and that year they actually ended up going on to win the state championship and I was still playing baseball but I wasn't on the varsity team, so that was, like, crushing for me because I was like, "Ah, you know what, if I would just have taken better care of myself, I would be on that varsity team, I'd have a championship ring" and I missed out on that because I didn't take care of myself and all those little details that went with it, so, that kind of got me going back to John at Xceleration.

I was like, "John, you know, I need to make some changes here" and then my family's also very supportive and they're

like, "Okay, we'll send you to a nutritionist" and then I started researching myself and then, boom, pretty much within three months I went from weighing 230 pounds, and this is, again, I have the perspective of almost losing too much and it was unhealthy, because I went to 155 pounds in about three months. So, that's an extreme weight loss, over 50 pounds, closer to 70 pounds in a three month timeframe. If you talk to any health professional, that's just not healthy.

I actually lost a little bit of hair, it came out. It came back, obviously, once you eat a little bit better but all these little factors, I have that firsthand experience and I educated myself and I wanted to learn, okay, how do I combat this aspect, how do I make it a lifestyle, not a three month crash diet where I'm going to lose all this weight but I'm also not going to feel as good and I learnt from there.

That's what got me into going to Stony Brook and developing and educating, but the one thing I kind of found was, my senior year I had lost both of my grandparents, that were basically like parents to me. This is the grandfather that got me into martial arts and the grandmother that basically took care of me and I was in a rough spot, you know, depression, the whole deal, so when I went to school, I wasn't fully prepared to be in college, I wasn't really willing to do the work and that kind of goes back to, when I talk to clients, you've got to be willing to do the work, be honest and be aware with yourself.

I wasn't being honest and I was being aware of myself, to saying "I shouldn't be in school right now, I should travel or train or do something else, I'm just wasting my time and I'm getting poor grades and all that fun stuff," but the benefit that came from it was that I found martial arts again. I got into Brazilian jiu-jitsu, which is a grappling art. That's what got me back into competitive fighting and then I ended up finding I'm actually kind of good at this.

My coach is like, "Listen, if you want to make a professional career out of this, this is what you should do, you have the athleticism, you're young enough, go for it, now's the time" so I listened to them and I had another great coach, I've had a bunch of great coaches, Eric Uresk was the mixed martial arts coach of where I was at. He's a professional fighter, he's retired now, and he actually lives in Thailand.

He's moved all over the world, he's been a big influence on my martial arts career and then Paul Rodriguez was my Brazilian jiu-jitsu coach and Mike Sanford, another Brazilian jiu-jitsu coach. They were very supportive of my goals and I ended up moving out to Las Vegas when I was 21 because I thought now's the time, right.

So, parents were supportive, we moved out there. I just became a certified personal trainer a couple of years prior, when I was 18. The second I could, I became certified and started working because I had a passion for it and even though I wasn't in school at that point, I was still educating myself, getting new certifications and I saw the lifestyle that these fighters had to live in Las Vegas.

I was training, I ran in Couture's gym at Xtreme Couture so anyone that knows mixed martial arts in the UFC world, because he's obviously a huge deal. He's a hall of fame fighter that's been retired now and will go down as maybe one of the best fighters in history, so getting to see the fighters that he had around him and the lifestyle they lived and the quality of life that they had to sacrifice to be able to be a part of that fighter lifestyle made me want to start my company.

That's when that happened and that's where it, kind of, cycled back around after a year of being out in Vegas. I miss my family, I'm a family guy, so I came back home, started going back to school, I re-educated myself, got my Associates Degree, started taking it back together with the company but also working in gyms.

I was working in gyms in Las Vegas so I've seen it from all different aspects and the biggest thing of all of that, that I kind of wanted to tie together that it's not like ... like I mentioned before, it's not just the physical. It's not just the mental. Martial arts, especially some of the best martial artists, and athletes in general, not just athletes.

Some of the most successful people in the world are able to tie the mental and the physical side of their bodies together, and that's what I've wanted to try and accomplish with the company.

What we're trying to do with our clients, that's what we continuously strive for, and with my education, that's what I try and do so my Associates was Exercise Science and then I went for my Bachelor's, kind of tied it with some sociology, so study mass society and some of the psychological habits with the business side of it because, obviously, you've got to be able to run a business and then the biology, so we understand the body.

Now I'm going for my Masters as a registered dietician and then for ... I do want to pursue a PhD after that in some form of clinical psychology or neuroscience, with the physiology of it, so I'm still trying to figure out that path.

But that's, kind of, I guess, the best way I can summarize my little bit of story, what, who am I, why, maybe, if anyone wants to listen to me, this is why I think my experience kind of helps me with my education and I can relate to a lot of people, for whether it's the depression side, whether it's the weight, whether it's body composition, even if you're an athlete, also I continuously compete now, I've been a fighter since.

Again, I like to think we're all fighters since I was a kid but I've been competing in mixed martial arts since 2010. I herniated a bunch of discs, I got eight herniation's throughout my back, four in my cervical, four in my lumbar and I've been able to actually work with my team from life as a fighter and doctors, different health professionals, physical therapists, John and his team over at Xceleration to get it down to two, one in my cervical, one in my lumbar and now I'm able to fight again, which is a dream for me because I thought I wasn't for a while.

I'm 29 now, so time is of the essence. I just recently won the Muay Thai championship at light-heavyweight for the WKA through Jackhammer Promotions, which was a huge goal for me and now the goal moving to Thailand, me and my fiancée, in June 2017 after we get married in April and then live out there for three months, immerse ourselves in the culture and continuously grow and share the perspectives with all of our audience, whoever wants to listen and anyone that we can help.

What would be your best piece of advice?

Mike Caulo: It's constantly seek discomfort and challenge yourself on a daily basis. And some days you will, some days you won't, and what I mean by that is, I think the most growth happens from being in a position where you're not comfortable.

It's easy to sit on the couch and be comfortable wrapped under a bunch of blankets and watch TV, or hang out with your friends but no one, I think, has ever achieved anything amazing from the couch under the blankets, unless nowadays with technology, laptops, a little different but for the most part, right, we're not going to really achieve anything in a comfort zone.

I think everyone needs to get uncomfortable and challenge themselves on a daily basis, which should be your goal. That's the biggest thing that I can leave everyone with.

Right. So, if there's anybody out there right now, Mike, how would they be able to find you, how would they be able to connect with you?

Mike Caulo: Yeah, the best way is going to our website at www.lifeofafighter.com.We have every bit of contact information, whether it's our phone numbers, our email account, and our social media. We have great articles and content under our blog. We have a bunch of free workouts and nutrition plans as well to get people, kind of, into the routine, get their feet wet, give them an idea of what we do. We have a preview of our ebook. We have all great stuff over there so I would definitely say the website's the best way for them to get in touch with us and get the ball rolling.

Is there anything that you'd like to share before you go?

Mike Caulo: What would you do if you knew failure wasn't an option? What would you try to accomplish, what would you go after, what kind of decisions in life would you make if you knew you weren't going to fail? Would you ask a girl out, would you go for a test, would you try and apply for a school, would you apply for a new job, would you take a fight, would you pursue an athletic endeavor? What would you do if you knew failure wasn't an option? I think that's the biggest thing I can leave everyone with.

ABOUT THE AUTHOR

Mark Imperial is a Best Selling Author, Syndicated Business Columnist, Syndicated Radio Host, and internationally recognized Stage, Screen, and Radio Host of numerous business shows spotlighting leading experts, entrepreneurs, and business celebrities.

His passion is discovering noteworthy business owners, professionals, experts, and leaders who do great work, and sharing their stories and secrets to their success with the world on his syndicated radio program titled "Remarkable Radio".

Mark is also the media marketing strategist and voice for some of the world's most famous brands. You can hear his voice over the airwaves weekly on Chicago radio and worldwide on iHeart Radio.

Mark is a Karate black belt, teaches kickboxing, loves Thai food, House Music, and his favorite TV show is infomercials.

Learn more:

www.MarkImperial.com
www.ImperialAction.com
www.RemarkableRadioShow.com

www.ingramcontent.com/pod-product-compliance
Lightning Source LLC
Chambersburg PA
CBHW072251270326
41930CB00010B/2340